BUILDING A HIGH-IMPACT BOARD-SUPERINTENDENT PARTNERSHIP

BUILDING A HIGH-IMPACT BOARD-SUPERINTENDENT PARTNERSHIP

11 Critical Questions You Need to Answer

Doug Eadie

ROWMAN & LITTLEFIELD
Lanham • Boulder • New York • London

Published by Rowman & Littlefield
An imprint of The Rowman & Littlefield Publishing Group, Inc.
4501 Forbes Boulevard, Suite 200, Lanham, Maryland 20706
www.rowman.com

6 Tinworth Street, London SE11 5AL

Copyright © 2019 by Doug Eadie

All rights reserved. No part of this book may be reproduced in any form or by any electronic or mechanical means, including information storage and retrieval systems, without written permission from the publisher, except by a reviewer who may quote passages in a review.

British Library Cataloguing in Publication Information Available

Library of Congress Cataloging-in-Publication Data Available

ISBN 978-1-4758-4786-4 (cloth)
ISBN 978-1-4758-4787-1 (pbk.)
ISBN 978-1-4758-4791-8 (electronic)

To my wife, Barbara Carlson Krai

CONTENTS

Foreword ix
Acknowledgments xiii

1 What's the State of the K–12 Governing Art? 1
2 What Exactly Do We Do When We Govern? 11
3 What Can Stand in the Way of High-Impact Governing? 21
4 What Is the Superintendent's Role in Governing? 31
5 How Can We Build a Solid Board-Superintendent Partnership? 41
6 What Does the Superintendent Do as Chief Board Developer? 55
7 How Can We Strengthen Our Board's Self-Management Capability? 69
8 How Can We Make Use of Board Standing Committees as Powerful Governing Engines? 83
9 How Can We Turn Board Members into Satisfied Owners of Their Planning Work? 95
10 How Can We Turn Board Members into Satisfied Owners of Their External/Stakeholder Relations Work? 107
11 How Can We Engage Senior Administrators in the Governing Process? 119

About the Author 131

FOREWORD

Doug Eadie's exciting new book makes a powerful contribution to the vitally important field of K–12 governance, and particularly to that most critical—and often fragile—partnership between the board of education and superintendent. Early in *Building a High-Impact Board-Superintendent Partnership*, Doug warns us that we are venturing into "frontier" territory that has not been fully explored. He correctly observes that K–12 governance is not a mature field with universally accepted principles and best practices. He counsels us to watch for—and guard against—what he calls "insidious foes" of a solid board-superintendent partnership: erroneous assumptions about aspects of governance that are insidious because they seem plausible at first blush. His example of one of these enemies of a solid partnership—the idea that there must be a firewall separating the "policy" role of the board from the executive-management role of the superintendent and senior administrators—really resonates with us since we passionately believe in close, creative collaboration with our boards.

Building a High-Impact Board-Superintendent Partnership is a unique book in several respects. First and foremost, it is not another abstract, theoretical look at the governing function in public education. Doug has drawn on his over thirty years of hands-on work with hundreds of public and nonprofit boards and chief executive officers, including a number of school boards and superintendents, in writing a book that is replete with practical, tested, real-world guidance aimed explicitly at school board members, superintendents, and district administrators. *Building a High-Impact Board-Superintendent Partnership* is to our knowledge the only book in the K–12 governance arena that provides educational leaders with a concrete definition of governing work that goes well beyond the old-time notion of governing as something vaguely called "policy making." Doug's definition of governing as making decisions about concrete governing "products" such as a values statement or annual budget and making judgments based on pertinent information such as a quarterly financial report comparing actual to budgeted expenditures is certainly borne out by our leadership experience. And as Doug points out, defining *governance* in this very concrete, down-to-earth fashion is the key to developing a board's governing capacity, since we must understand the nature of governing work before we can tackle how to do it well.

Building a High-Impact Board-Superintendent Partnership is also unique in its breadth. This compact but detail-rich book contains eleven chapters dealing with every important facet of K–12 governance, such as significant trends in this rapidly changing field, major barriers standing in the way of effective governing, the superintendent's role in the governing process, how to capitalize on well-designed committees as "governing engines," practical ways to meaningfully engage board members in the planning and external relations functions, and much more.

We wholeheartedly subscribe to the four core concepts that Doug tells us undergird the practical wisdom in his book. First, governing is a "team sport" played by what Doug calls the "Strategic Governing Team": the board of education; the superintendent; and district administrators. Second, the board can and must be systematically developed as a governing organization if it is to function at a high level. Third, board members must be actively engaged in shaping their governing decisions if they are to own, and be firmly committed to, these decisions. And fourth, the superintendent must serve as the de facto "captain" of the district's Strategic Governing Team if high-impact governing work is to be accomplished.

Whether you are a school board member, a superintendent, or a district administrator aspiring to take the helm of a school district at some point in your career, you will want to keep *Building a High-*

FOREWORD xi

Impact Board-Superintendent Partnership close at hand as a powerful resource you can draw on in carrying out your leadership mission.

With best wishes, your colleagues:

>Talisa Dixon, Superintendent
>Columbus City Schools
>Columbus, Ohio

>Susan Enfield, Superintendent
>Highline Public Schools
>Burien, Washington

>Gregory Hutchings, Superintendent
>Alexandria City Public Schools
>Alexandria, Virginia

>Bryan Luizzi, Superintendent
>New Canaan Public Schools
>New Canaan, Connecticut

>Oliver Robinson, Superintendent
>Shenendehowa Central School District
>Clifton Park, New York

>David Schuler, Superintendent
>Township High School District 214
>Arlington Heights, Illinois

>Aaron Spence, Superintendent
>Virginia Beach City Public Schools
>Virginia Beach, Virginia

ACKNOWLEDGMENTS

I cannot take sole credit for the concepts, principles, and practices that I write about in *Building a High-Impact Board-Superintendent Partnership*. In this regard, I deeply appreciate what I have learned from the many school board members, superintendents, and district administrators I have worked with over the past thirty years about the art of governing and building solid board-superintendent partnerships. They are in a real sense my co-authors.

My knowledge in the rapidly developing field of public/nonprofit governance has been enriched by the penetrating questions and thoughtful observations of the hundreds of participants in the workshops I have conducted over the years, making this book a more powerful resource for K–12 leaders who aspire to build their boards' governing capacity and take their board-superintendent partnership to the next level. I am especially indebted to Dan Domenech, executive director, and his executive team at the American Association of School Administrators, and Thomas Gentzel, executive director and CEO, and his executive team at the National School Boards Association, for providing me with so many opportunities to present workshops on K–12 board and superintendent leadership over the past three decades.

I am also indebted to the K–12 leaders serving on the Strategic Advisory Committee of the national K–12 blog my company manages, www.boardsavvysuperintendent.com, who have worked closely with me in building a rich reservoir of information on K–12 leadership through their podcasts and posts and who reviewed and commented on my writing outline for this book. Thanks so much for your contribution to this book and my blog and to the cause of K–12 board and superintendent leadership: Gary Amoroso, executive director, Minnesota Association of School Administrators; Rosa Atkins, superintendent, Charlottesville City Schools (Virginia); Luvelle Brown, superintendent, Ithaca City School District (New York); Gillian Chapman, superintendent, Teton County School District #1 (Wyoming); Jeff Dillon, superintendent, Wilder School District (Idaho); Talisa Dixon, superintendent, Columbus City Schools (Ohio); Susan Enfield, superintendent, Highline Public Schools (Washington); Jose Espinoza, superintendent, Socorro Independent School District (Texas); Gregory Hutchings, superintendent, Alexandria City Public Schools (Virginia); Lisa Karmacharya, executive director, Mississippi Association of School Administrators; Michael Lubelfeld, superintendent, Deerfield Public School District 109 (Illinois); Bryan Luizzi, superintendent, New Canaan Public Schools (Connecticut); Khalid Mumin, superintendent, Reading School District (Pennsylvania); Steve Murley, superintendent, Iowa City Community School District (Iowa); Gina Patterson, executive director, Virginia School Boards Association; David Pennington, superintendent, Ponca City Schools (Oklahoma); Nick Polyak, superintendent, Leyden Community High School District #212 (Illinois); Robert Rader, executive director, Connecticut Association of Boards of Education; Oliver Robinson, superintendent, Shenendehowa Central School District (New York); David Schuler, superintendent, Township High School District 214 (Illinois); Mort Sherman, associate executive director, American Association of School Administrators; Lloyd Snow, superintendent, Sand Springs Public Schools (Oklahoma); Aaron Spence, superintendent, Virginia Beach City Public Schools (Virginia); and Chris Wigent, executive director, Michigan Association of School Administrators.

I highly value my association with Rowman & Littlefield, the publisher of this and my other K–12 leadership books, and I am especially grateful to Tom Koerner, vice president and publisher, and Carlie Wall, managing editor, for their support and encouragement during the writing of this book.

Finally, I could not have written nearly as good a book while juggling the demands of four national blogs, frequent speaking engagements, and my national governance consulting practice without the strong encouragement, patience, and unfailing support of my wife, best friend, and close business associate, Barbara Carlson Krai. Thank you, Barbara!

1

WHAT'S THE STATE OF THE K–12 GOVERNING ART?

WHY I WROTE THIS BOOK

No work could possibly be more important than educating young people—helping them to thrive over the course of their lives in a rapidly changing, always challenging world, to realize their tremendous potential as fully as possible in the time they've been granted. The governance function in education is not an end in itself; it is intended to serve this ultimate purpose of building productive, satisfying, principled lives. I wrote this book because a quarter-century of experience has taught me that governance is a critical path to educational excellence and student achievement—that governing performance is one of the preeminent drivers of educational performance. The governing decisions and judgments that your school board makes, in collaboration with your superintendent and senior administrators—such as adopting an updated values and vision statement for your district, setting district strategic goals and operational targets, and adopting next year's budget—have a tremendous impact on your district's long-range educational performance in terms of student achievement, and on your district's financial health and institutional stability.

I also undertook this book because I have learned from experience that the school board members, superintendents, and senior administrators who are accountable for the governing function sorely need up-to-date, tested, and practical information that will help them govern at a high level. Experience has taught me that many, if not most, board members arrive at the district boardroom lacking the knowledge and skills to govern well, and that having to spend a year or more learning the governing ropes comes at a steep price in terms of not only reduced board effectiveness, but also frustrated, dissatisfied board members who have been known to take their frustration out on the superintendent. I have also learned that many, if not most, superintendents arrive at the top spot in their districts ill-prepared to play a leading role in developing their board's governing capability and in building and maintaining a close and positive working relationship with the board, reducing board effectiveness, frustrating board members, and all too often threatening the superintendent's tenure. Unfortunately, not only are comprehensive, detailed courses on the K–12 governing function and the board-superintendent working relationship largely absent in graduate schools of education, but aspiring superintendents are also highly unlikely to acquire much practical governing knowledge as they climb up the district organizational ladder on their way to the superintendent's office.

THIS BOOK'S PRACTICAL VALUE TO YOU

This book is intended to be a down-to-earth, nuts-and-bolts resource that you—whether you're a school board member, superintendent, or senior administrator—can rely on in charting your course in an incredibly high-stakes, dauntingly complex and often professionally perilous leadership arena: K–12 governance. This book is about the detailed governing work that high-performing school boards do and about the board-superintendent partnership that is at the heart of what we call "high-impact" governing: important governing decisions and judgments that make a significant difference in the affairs of your school district. This is not an academic or theoretical book, nor is it another one of those abstract surveys of the literature. Rather, this book is chock full of detailed, practical guidance that has been thoroughly tested in all kinds of real-life situations. My aim is to arm you with pertinent information that you can put to immediate use in strengthening your board's governing performance and in building a really solid board-superintendent partnership that can withstand the inevitable stresses and strains at the top of all school districts.

If you're a school board member, this book will enrich your understanding of what the demanding, highly complex work of governing is all about and the steps you need to take—working closely with your superintendent and his or her top lieutenants—to ensure a productive, stimulating, and thoroughly satisfying boardroom experience. It will help you go light years beyond the old-time passive-reactive model that has trapped so many board members in the dispiriting process of thumbing through and reacting to finished staff work. You deserve a more powerful return on your investment of time and energy in governing, and this book will help you realize that return on investment. If you're a superintendent, this book will help you and your senior administrators fashion and execute strategies for developing your board into a higher-performing governing body—with a clearer governing role, better defined governing functions, and updated governing structure and processes. You can also rely on this book to help you build and maintain a close, productive, and enduring working relationship with your school.

SETTING THE STAGE FOR WHAT FOLLOWS

The first three chapters of this book set the stage for the following eight chapters, each of which addresses a high-stakes question that must be answered in building a truly high-impact school board-superintendent partnership that is characterized by strong governing performance and a solid board-superintendent working relationship. This opening chapter sets the stage for the following chapters by examining the state of the governing art in this country at this point in time, describing a function—not a fully developed field—that is rapidly evolving and that is filled with wrong-headed wisdom that can reduce your board's governing effectiveness while also jeopardizing your superintendent's partnership with the board. This first chapter also takes a look at emerging trends that augur well for the future of K–12 governance in this country.

The second chapter examines the actual work your school board and the other members of your district's "Strategic Governing Team"—your superintendent and senior administrators—do when they govern, going well beyond the outdated notion of governing being something called "policy making," and also describes four core concepts at the heart of effective governing. The third chapter describes several challenges that stand in the way of strong governing performance and a solid board-superintendent partnership and introduces the keys to meeting these challenges, which are dealt with in detail in the following eight chapters.

WELCOME TO THE FRONTIER

"Raise your hand if you've had a really comprehensive, nuts-and-bolts course in graduate school on the work of governing, the roles of the school board and superintendent in the governing process, and ways to build a maintain a really solid board-superintendent partnership?" I open every one of my governing workshops for board members, chief executives, and senior administrators—most recently at the AASA and NSBA 2018 annual meetings—by asking this question. Never more than two or three hands go up, typically none. Welcome to the governing frontier! Despite the fact that governing boards have been a fact of life since the beginning of our republic—earlier in the case of the New England colonies—at this point in our country's history you would not say that public/nonprofit governance generally, and K–12 governance specifically, is a full-fledged field with the universal agreement on core principles and best practices that characterizes a mature field.

Instead, K–12 governance is a developing field—actually more of a leadership function—that is in a state of constant flux and is marked by often-heated debate about the principles that should guide the governing process and the practices that should be followed in making governing decisions and judgments. This lack of cohesion means, of course, that governing can be dangerous terrain, not so much for school boards, but for the superintendents working for and with them. Over my quarter-century of work with hundreds of board members and chief executives such as superintendents, I've come across a number of what I call "insidious foes" of governing board performance and of the board-superintendent partnership. These are erroneous assumptions about aspects of the governing process that can significantly limit a board's governing effectiveness and erode the board-superintendent partnership. What makes them insidious is that they can sound plausible and are even frequently promoted by self-styled governing gurus.

LET "CAVEAT EMPTOR" BE YOUR WATCHWORD

A common example of an insidious foe that you're well-advised to avoid is the wrong-headed notion that a fire wall should separate the so-called "policy-making" work of the board from the completely different work that chief executives such as superintendents and their executive team members do. The twain should not be allowed to meet, firewall proponents say, and a major responsibility of the chief executive is to preserve the wall as the best way to fend off micromanaging board members who are all-too-often tempted to meddle in executive and administrative details. Of course, as many if not most of my readers well know, the twain always meet since the process of making governing decisions and judgments requires the in-depth, creative collaboration of board members, superintendents, and their senior administrators spending lots of time at the same table.

Over the years, I've seen more than one chief executive, including a number of superintendents, come to grief, professionally speaking, by paying more attention to fending off board micromanagement than to fostering the kind of intensive board-executive collaboration that is at the heart of effective governing. Really board-savvy superintendents know that the absence of creative board-superintendent collaboration inevitably leads to frustrated, dissatisfied board members who tend to take their frustration out on the superintendent. I'll never forget a few years ago being contacted by a board chair and superintendent who wanted to discuss a serious problem they were facing. "We're in a state of shock and can't figure out what's going on." These were the first words I recall coming out of the board president's mouth in the conference call she and her superintendent had scheduled with me.

They went on to explain that seven months ago the school board, superintendent, and his district administrative cabinet had completed a comprehensive governance policy review and update and had compiled the updated policies in a board manual that had been unanimously adopted by the board. They explained that for the first time they'd assembled what they called the "governing rules of the game" in one, well-organized policy book. They told me that they'd spent hours distinguishing between the board's and superintendent's primary responsibilities—"most importantly," they said, spelling out the superintendent's "executive limitations." By the way, it turned out that they'd invested a hefty amount in the project, not only in consulting fees but also the cost of over a hundred hours of board and staff time spent deliberating in work sessions and drafting new and updated governing policies.

Having listened for fifteen minutes or so, I asked why they'd called me. Well, it turns out that in the seven months since putting their governing rules of the game in place, the board-superintendent-executive cabinet working relationship had gone steadily downhill. There was lots of carping at monthly board business meetings, the last budget-preparation process had been excruciatingly painful—with lots of nitpicking in what seemed like interminable budget review sessions—and the superintendent said she was wondering if her job was in jeopardy. I recall the anguish in her voice when she asked how they'd gotten to this point after diligently doing so much good work. My on-the-spot diagnosis—based on encounters with many similar situations over the years—was that they'd probably focused exclusively on getting the rules of the game established. However, they hadn't paid equal attention to an even more important task: putting in place and/or fine-tuning the governing structure and processes that would make active board member engagement in key governing areas such as annual operational planning and educational performance monitoring possible. It was pretty obvious to me that they'd been seduced by the siren song of an old-fashioned, dangerously simplistic, hopelessly incomplete board capacity-building approach commonly known as "policy governance," and they were paying the price.

IMPORTANT DEVELOPMENTS IN THE GOVERNING ARENA

We can take advantage of a number of important developments in the K–12 governing arena in building our school board's governing capacity and strengthening the board-superintendent partnership. I'll bring this opening chapter to a close by taking a brief look at five of the more consequential recent developments that augur well for the future of K–12 governance: the appearance of a new breed of board member who expects to make a real difference in the short-term; a growing number of superintendents who welcome strong board leadership and collaboration on the governing front; the slow but sure decline of the traditional passive-reactive governing model; growing acceptance of intensive board interaction with senior administrators reporting to the superintendent; and a sense of acute crisis in public education.

New Breed of Board Member

"From day one on the board, I expected to hit the ground running. I know life is too short to sit around the table as a kind of quiet observer for six months or so while I'm learning the ropes. I was elected to make a difference, and I intend to—now, not a year from now!" This from a board member in her first week on her new governing job, responding to my question why she'd run for the board and what she expected to accomplish. These days I frequently hear such comments when I'm interviewing new board members. Twenty years ago, I could count on one hand the incoming board members who were so impatient to make an impact. Far more common in those days, in my experience, were board members who understood that in their first year on the board they should generally keep quiet, pay close attention to more senior board colleagues, and eventually learn enough to play a more active and assertive governing role. No more! Instant governing gratification appears to be the name of the new governing game.

This growing impatience is good news in the sense that it creates healthy pressure on superintendents and longer-tenured board members to systematically upgrade their boards' governing capacity to ensure that all board members, including the impatient newcomers, are actively engaged in making a difference in their districts. This means clarifying the board's governing role and functions, developing the board's structure (mainly well-designed board committees), and updating processes for meaningful engagement. The bad news is that superintendents who don't play an assertive role in the board capacity-building process are highly likely to alienate impatient board members, turning them into potentially dangerous adversaries.

Board Savvier Superintendents

I'm also seeing significant growth in the number of superintendents who are avidly interested in the governing function, who view board members as a valuable district asset, see governing as one of their top priorities, and welcome strong board leadership and a collaborative working relationship. This new breed of superintendent is the polar opposite of the old-style K–12 chief executive who keeps a wary distance from the board, believes that there really should be a firewall separating board "policy making" from executive/administrative management, and is always on the defensive, guarding against possible board micromanagement. What I'm not seeing, even now, is an increasing number of superintendents who arrive in the top spot in the district equipped with the knowledge and skills they need to take the lead in building their board's governing capacity and a solid board-superintendent working relationship. But what I am seeing is a new openness to collaboration with the board and a keen appetite for nuts-and-bolts information on the work of governing and partnership building.

Steady Decline of the Passive-Reactive Model

The passive-reactive governance model—which in a nutshell defines governing as largely a process of board members reviewing and reacting to finished staff work such as a budget document—is, I'm sorry to say, still alive, although definitely on the wane. For one thing, newcomers on school boards around the country are increasingly far less inclined to spend much of their time thumbing through finished documents, as noted above. For another, a growing number of superintendents have gotten the message that board members who are satisfied owners of their governing work make for more reliable partners with—and supporters of—the superintendent, and that such ownership is fostered by active engagement, not mere reaction.

So the passive-reactive model is on the way out, but don't underestimate the emotional attachment to the traditional approach, especially among senior administrators and managers, who for years and years have grown comfortable with the document-centered process and don't welcome the prospect of board engagement with open arms. I recently sat in on a daylong work session at which a superintendent and his senior administrators reviewed recommendations for engaging board members in shaping—not merely reacting to—such critical governing products as an updated vision statement, a set of annual operational objects, and the annual budget, and discussed how to implement the objectives. The apprehension in the room was palpable.

Board Interaction with Senior Administrators

There's growing recognition that interaction between board members and senior administrators reporting to the superintendent is healthy, not only in formal settings like a strategic planning work session or a governance improvement retreat, but also in day-to-day affairs. In the governance realm, in my experience, familiarity breeds understanding and respect and facilitates the kind of bonding that fosters collaboration. These days the traditional idea that all board communication with senior administrators should flow through the bottleneck of the superintendent's office is rightly being questioned. For one thing, it's very cumbersome. For another, it serves no useful purpose. However, as I'll discuss in chapter 5, allowing free communication and interaction will only work well if constrained by clear guidelines and carefully monitored. For example, one common guideline is that a board member can request routine information from an administrator, but not information that isn't easily available, and no board member can actually assign a project to an administrator.

The Widespread Perception of Crisis

It may be an exaggeration to say that public school districts around the country are under siege, but no reader is likely to disagree that public education is being challenged on a number of fronts, including the proliferation of competitive educational delivery systems such as charter schools, negative media attention, and cutbacks in state education budgets. The widespread perception that public education is in a crisis is serving a number of useful purposes: for example, serious attention to the very important business of image building (as they say, either create your own positive image, or have others create a negative one for you) and a growing investment in innovation to enhance performance. On the governance front, the perception of crisis is elevating the importance of school boards, whose governing decisions and nongoverning public relations and image-building efforts are rightly seen as critical to district success, and is resulting in serious attention to school board capacity building.

2

WHAT EXACTLY DO WE DO WHEN WE GOVERN?

This chapter takes a close look at the nuts and bolts work K–12 Strategic Governing Teams (the school board, superintendent, and superintendent's administrative team) do when they govern well, briefly describes the nongoverning work often done by school boards, and acquaints readers with four core concepts that undergird the guidance I provide in this book.

GOVERNING AT THE HIGHEST LEVEL

What does this very special organization we call a governing board actually do when it governs your district? At this highest level, the board answers three critical questions continuously—over and over again, working in close partnership with your superintendent and senior administrative team:

1. *Where should our district be headed, and what should it become over the long run?* What is our vision in terms of the range of educational programs and services we will be providing, the values that should guide us in providing these services, the capital investment and revenues from various sources that will be required to deliver these services, and the like? This is what we

might call the strategic question, and your board answers this question by engaging in some kind of strategic planning process.

2. *What is our district in the short run: right now and over the coming year?* What is our mission in terms of the educational programs and services we are providing and the students we serve? What are our operational priorities and our educational and managerial targets? What is our current and next year's budget? What is the image we want to convey—what messages do we want to send: to our students, their families, the public at large, and key stakeholders? The questions making up this overall short-term question are answered through your board's involvement in some kind of operational planning and budget-preparation process.

3. *How are we doing?* This is what you might call the accountability question, which is always of great interest to our students' parents, the other taxpayers who fund our educational programs and services, and key stakeholder organizations. Are we meeting our operational performance targets? Are we managing our financial and other resources well? Are our administrative systems up to date and functioning satisfactorily? Are we attracting and retaining qualified employees? Are we conveying the image we intend to convey? The specific questions making up this broad accountability question are answered by your board making judgments based on reviewing educational and financial performance reports, community surveys, and input from key stakeholder organizations.

DRILLING DOWN

Now, let's drill down, defining the board's governing work less abstractly and more concretely. What is the nuts-and-bolts work of governing? Over my quarter-century of hands-on involvement with a wide variety of governing boards, I've frequently heard governing described as "policy making." When you think about it, this can't possibly be a complete answer. Policies are broad rules to govern your school district's—and also your board's—operations. Only the most important, highest-stakes rules require your board's attention:

how contracts are entered into, who can authorize different levels of expenditures, how employee evaluation should be done, etc. There aren't all that many policies requiring your board's attention, so it really doesn't make sense to say that "policy making" is basically what your board does when it governs. So what is the detailed work of governing?

Experience has taught me that all public/nonprofit boards, including school boards, are essentially decision-making and judgment-making governing bodies. School boards make very specific decisions about concrete governing "products," and they make judgments based on reviewing pertinent information. These governing decisions and judgments tend to flow along three broad streams: planning—both strategic and operational (including budget preparation); performance monitoring; and external/stakeholder relations. For example, swimming in the planning stream, school boards make decisions about such governing "products" as an updated values and vision statement, strategic goals, and the annual operating plan and budget.

Swimming in the performance-monitoring stream, school boards make judgments about educational and financial performance based on their review of performance reports and other data. And swimming in the external/stakeholder relations stream, school boards make decisions about the key messages making up your district's desired image and about its public, stakeholder, and legislative relations strategies. We don't want to get ahead of ourselves, but if you agree with the widely accepted management principle that structure should reflect—and be aligned with—function, then we have the makings of a well-designed board committee structure that I'll describe in detail later in this book.

YOUR BOARD'S NONGOVERNING WORK

Later in this book I'll deal in detail with the nongoverning work that school board members are frequently engaged in doing, which is in my experience often quite important. For example, many school board members, working closely with the superintendent and senior administrators, often engage in creative image building for their district, primarily by speaking in such community forums as Rotary and chamber of commerce luncheons and civic association meetings, talking about their district's mission, programs, financing, educational performance, and the like. Board members also frequently participate in legislative briefings at the state capital and "on the hill" in Washington. And school board members can be a valuable resource in maintaining relationships with such key stakeholders as the mayor's office, city council, county commission, regional planning agency, and the like.

There's nothing wrong with board members engaging in such important nongoverning work, but it should never be allowed to overshadow or impinge on your board's "Job #1": making the governing decisions and judgments that are critical to your district's carrying out its educational mission fully and cost-effectively and to its future stability. Is there a clear and present danger that board members' nongoverning work might interfere with their governing performance? Absolutely, for the simple reason that speaking and stakeholder relationship management is very straightforward, easy-to-understand work that can be quite ego satisfying, while governing can be tremendously complex and painful (e.g., when trimming budgets, consolidating buildings, putting a tax issue on the ballot, and the like) and can feel abstract and distant.

FOUR CORE CONCEPTS AT THE HEART OF THIS BOOK

Four core concepts undergird the practical guidance that I share in the following nine chapters:

1. Governing at a high level is a team sport played by the members of what we call the "Strategic Governing Team."
2. Your board can—and must—be systematically developed if it is to govern at a high level.
3. Board members must be actively engaged in shaping their governing decisions and judgments if they are to own—and be firmly committed to—their decisions and judgments.
4. The superintendent must be the de facto captain of your district's Strategic Governing Team.

GOVERNING IS A TEAM SPORT

As I observed in chapter 1, the old-time notion of a firewall separating the so-called "policy-making" role of the board from the executive management and administrative work of the superintendent and senior administrative team might sound good in theory, but as most of my readers no doubt know, it breaks down in practice. I learned early in my work with boards and their CEOs that governing is truly a team sport. Boards can't carry the governing burden alone for obvious reasons: limited time (the great majority of board members having full lives outside of the board); lack of governing expertise; the need for detailed information on your district's educational and managerial operations; and the like. So you can think of governing as the shared responsibility of the members of what I call the Strategic Governing Team: the school board; the superintendent; and the senior administrators reporting to the superintendent. Creative collaboration characterizes the governing game, where the "we-they" mentality has no place. In my experience, almost all of the really important decisions and judgments that make up the work of governing are shaped by the members of the Strategic Governing Team sitting around the table—typically in board committee meetings and special work sessions—before the final decisions and judgments are made in the full board business meeting.

THE CASE FOR BOARD ORGANIZATIONAL DEVELOPMENT

You might not have thought about it in this way, but your school board is essentially an organizational unit within your overall district organization, along with other organizational units like the office of the superintendent, the finance and human resources departments, the curriculum and instruction unit, and individual buildings. Like all other organizational units making up your district, the school board is a formally established, permanent organization that—through formal structure and process—carries out a specific mission: governing your district. Why does it matter? Well, as an organization rather than an abstract concept, your school board can—and must—be systematically developed to enable it to carry out its governing mission more fully: by developing the people making up the board; clarifying and refining the board's role and functions; updating and fine-tuning its structure; and developing the processes it employs in governing. Or you can take the inheritance route: merely projecting today's and yesterday's board into the future. Since you've starting reading this book, you presumably have eschewed the inheritance option, choosing instead to systematically develop your board's governing capacity.

Governing is a high-stakes function. Systematically developing your board as a governing organization will reap handsome dividends for your district, and failing to build your board's governing capacity can come at a steep cost. For example:

- Over the long-run, your district's educational effectiveness and financial stability depend more than any other factor on the governing decisions your board makes when it is engaged in strategic and operational planning and annual budget preparation and on the judgments board members make when wearing their performance oversight and monitoring hat. What's at stake is not only your students' achievement, but also your district's image and public support for financing existing operations and expansion initiatives. A reputation for lackluster educational and managerial performance is a sure-fire recipe for defeat at the polls in my experience.
- Your district's image and level of public support depend not only on its educational and managerial performance but also on the board's credibility as a governing body. If your board is seen as essentially a rubber stamp for finished staff work or, worse, as a dysfunctional governing family, with constant bickering and backbiting, then public support will inevitably erode over time.
- And the partnership between your school board and superintendent is also impacted by the board's governing performance. Experience has taught that board members who are actively engaged in doing high-impact governing work that makes an obvious difference in the affairs of their district tend to feel a high degree of ownership and satisfaction that makes them more reliable partners for the superintendent. By contrast, board members who find their governing work frustrating and unsatisfying tend to place the blame squarely on the superintendent. As a former an-

cient history teacher, I can say with assurance that since the time of the great Egyptian Pharaoh Amenhotep III, no board in the world has been known to punish, much less fire, itself for the frustration resulting from its underperformance!

MEANINGFUL BOARD MEMBER ENGAGEMENT IS KEY TO OWNERSHIP AND COMMITMENT

The traditional passive-reactive model of governing—characterized by the superintendent and senior administrative team members sending finished documents to the board, which then thumbs through them (what I think of as the "thumbing through" approach to policy making) is now the exception to the rule in public/nonprofit governance, for three very compelling reasons. First, the passive-reactive approach lacks the kind of intensive board-superintendent-senior administrative team interaction—the back-and-forth questioning and in-depth discussion that lead to well-informed decision making. Second, the traditional model fails to capitalize on board members as a precious asset—their diverse experience, expertise in pertinent fields such as financial management, strategic planning, and marketing, their varied perspectives, and their connections to key stakeholders. And third, the passive-reactive approach turns board members into an audience with little, if any, ownership of, and commitment to, the decisions they make.

The practical alternative to the waning passive-reactive model is to systematically engage board members in well-designed processes that enable them to shape their governing decisions and judgments, thereby transforming them into committed owners of their governing work rather than a mere audience for finished staff work. For example, as I discuss in detail later in this book, actively engaging board members early in your district's strategic planning process in updating your district's values and vision and in identifying the major issues—both challenges and opportunities—that deserve serious board attention is a sure-fire way to build board commitment to your updated strategic plan. And engaging your board members in updating the content and format of the educational and financial performance reports they regularly receive is a reliable way to foster commitment to their oversight and monitoring role and the judgments they make on the basis of these reports.

THE CEO AS CAPTAIN OF THE STRATEGIC GOVERNING TEAM

When a school board chooses its superintendent, it's also choosing the de facto captain of the Strategic Governing Team. Governing really is a collaborative venture, involving intensive, well-orchestrated teamwork to ensure that the decisions and judgments that constitute governing work are made in a full and timely fashion. Your school board is obviously the most senior member of the Strategic Governing Team—the ultimate authority, judge, and decision maker. However, your superintendent has to wear the team captain hat in practice, if not theory, if you want the Strategic Governing Team to be healthy, cohesive, and productive. The reason is simple: time—the superintendent's and senior administrative team's—and access to resources. No matter how capable, committed, and dedicated board members might be—and experience has taught me that they typically are—the fact is that the great majority are part-time, unpaid volunteers. Only the superintendent has the time (including senior staff's) to plan for, manage, and support the Strategic Governing Team.

The superintendents who function most effectively as de facto captains of their district's Strategic Governing Teams, as I discuss later in this book in considerable detail, are highly board-savvy. Who are these board-savvy superintendents?

- First and foremost, they bring a very positive and constructive attitude to their work with their boards, seeing the board as both a close colleague and partner in leading and a precious organizational resource. Seeing the board-staff relationship in "we-they" terms is alien to the board-savvy superintendent.
- Board-savvy superintendents believe that governing is one of the highest-priority, top-tier chief executive functions, albeit shared with their board, and they put their money where their mouth is, devoting significant time and attention to becoming

experts in governing and to managing and supporting the governing function.
- They enthusiastically wear the "chief board developer" hat in their district, embracing systematic board capacity building as one of their critical superintendent responsibilities and taking explicit responsibility for making it happen.
- These board-savvy superintendents pay close attention to the emotional and psychological dimension of their chief board developer role, always on the lookout for ways to strengthen board members' ownership of their governing work and to provide them with ego satisfaction.

3

WHAT CAN STAND IN THE WAY OF HIGH-IMPACT GOVERNING?

HIGH-IMPACT GOVERNING IS NEVER A PIECE OF CAKE

The members of this southwestern district's Strategic Governing Team—the school board, superintendent, and her administrative cabinet—were ecstatic but exhausted. The night before, at their regular monthly business meeting, school board members had made a high-stakes governing decision: to implement an innovation initiative to consolidate two elementary schools in response to a significant drop in school-age children over the prior five years that was expected to continue for the foreseeable future. Mission accomplished! But the cost in top-level time had been pretty steep over the course of some nine months.

The innovation initiative was born in a daylong retreat involving all members of the Strategic Governing Team, who red-flagged the population drop and the issue of two underutilized elementary buildings. Deciding to make this a top-priority matter, the team put in place a task force to flesh out a strategy addressing the issue, consisting of two of the nine board members, three district office administrators, the principals of the two buildings, and the presidents of the two buildings' parent-teacher organizations. Because of the stakes involved—including not only money but also the district's reputation—a consultant was retained to provide technical advice and facilitate task force deliberations. After three months of diligent work, the task force presented its strategy at two PTO meetings and after some tweaking to the full school board in a three-hour work session. A month later, at the regular board business meeting, the trustees voted unanimously to implement the consolidation strategy. This is high-impact governing in action.

Of course, not everything that goes on in board committee meetings and in your district boardroom is this complex and demanding. There are always consent items on the board agenda that don't require serious attention because they're fairly routine—for example, approving a long list of faculty appointments for the coming school year and reviewing contracts for items already in your district's budget. And board agendas typically include a steady stream of for-information-only briefings that don't call for action. But what I call "high-impact" governing is—even under the most favorable of circumstances, when the stars are perfectly aligned—an extremely challenging process, which is no doubt why we don't typically see droves of candidates vying for seats on school boards around the country.

High-impact governing, you'll recall, involves actively engaging board members in shaping and making decisions and judgments that significantly impact the affairs of your school district. By definition, high-impact governing work has to do with complex, high-stakes matters that aren't amenable to simple solutions: updating your district's vision and core values, establishing long-range goals and annual performance targets, adopting the annual budget, dealing with educational performance shortfalls and inadequate financial resources, and the like. And the barriers to high-impact governing work can seem pretty daunting, including lingering allegiance to the outmoded passive-reactive governing model; counterproductive attitudes; insufficient governing knowledge and skills; underdeveloped school board composition; the centrifugal force affecting the board; and the absence of board organizational development. This chapter briefly examines each of these six barriers and then describes the keys to surmounting them, which are covered in detail in the following eight chapters of this book.

LINGERING ALLEGIANCE TO THE PASSIVE-REACTIVE MODEL

My consulting work with K–12 Strategic Governing Teams over the past quarter-century has often involved spending a day near the end of an engagement with the superintendent and her top administrators. These daylong work sessions typically focus on the implementation of recommendations to strengthen the school board's governing performance and the board-superintendent-senior administrative team working relationship. They emerged from a daylong Strategic Governing Team retreat a few weeks earlier—for example, to put in place a well-designed board standing committee structure and processes for the board to oversee its own governing performance and to manage its partnership with the superintendent.

Sitting in on the most recent K–12 superintendent-administrator implantation strategy session a couple of weeks ago, I expected—and so wasn't surprised by—several administrators' strong push-back on two of the most consequential recommendations: first, to engage board members in a meaningful way in shaping important governing decisions, rather than treating them like an audience for finished staff work; and second, the use of well-designed board committees as engagement vehicles. For the umpteenth time, I could feel a pervasive sense of anxiety and apprehension in the room. The feeling of dread was, as usual, palpable. At this point in my career as a governance advisor, I well understood that the apprehension and resistance had to do with fear that board members' heightened engagement would lead to rampant micromanagement.

It wasn't that these bright, very capable administrators thought the traditional passive-reactive model was all that great. But at least it served, in their minds, as a bulwark against micromanaging board members' tentacles wrapping around nongoverning, purely executive and administrative functions. The passive-reactive model was clearly the lesser of two evils to many of the administrators in the room: a reactive board of nonowners rather than ardent micromanagers. The obvious solution is to allay such fears by getting into the actual details and demonstrating how the heightened engagement would actually work against micromanagement. But the point is that you should never underestimate the resistance you are likely to encounter in any effort to substitute stronger board engagement for the old-time passive-reactive model.

COUNTERPRODUCTIVE ATTITUDES

Over the years, I've seen many superintendents and school board members bring counterproductive attitudes to their governing work that can seriously impede the development of the board's governing capacity and the board-superintendent working relationship. This is very typical of newly minted district chief executives and recently elected board members, but I've often seen the attitudes persist well into their tenures, at the expense of high-impact governing work (and in the case of superintendents, sad to say, frequently an emphatic invitation to take their skills to another district). In the case of these superintendents, what's at work is a negative perception of the school board as not a precious asset, but rather a threat posing a clear and present danger to superintendent prerogatives. Since, as I observed earlier in this book, many if not most superintendent-aspirants do not learn much about governing dynamics and board-superintendent relationship management prior to taking the CEO helm in a district, they can all too easily arrive at the top spot with their fears intact.

It wasn't too long ago that, over lunch with a superintendent six months into her new job, I mentioned what a wonderful opportunity the annual budget-preparation process would be for engaging board members in providing front-end substantive guidance before actually cranking out a budget with all the numbers filled in. Her immediate reaction was a glacial glare as she informed me that her job was to produce the budget, and her board's was to review it. End of story! I'm pleased to report that over the course of our long lunch her fears were largely allayed, as we discussed concrete and safe ways to engage board members—for example, by holding a pre-budget Strategic Governing Team work session (involving the board, superintendent, and senior administrators) at which team members would reach consensus on the operational issues deserving special attention in the budget. It seemed obvious to me, until I reflected on this superintendent's never having experienced such a session on her way up the administrative ladder.

On the board side of the governing equation, the most entrenched and pernicious bad attitude that I've seen impede collaboration in doing high-impact governing work is what I call "watch-the-critters-so-they-don't-steal-the-store." Widespread and apparently growing suspicion of public institutions ensures that this inherently adversarial attitude will continue to pollute the boardrooms of countless districts. Experience has taught me that it can be overcome and replaced by a more collaborative attitude, but only with considerable thought, carefully conceived strategy, and concentrated effort. Education of board members—providing them with case studies of board-superintendent-administrator collaboration in making important governing decisions—has proved to be very helpful. Many superintendents have also taken the lead in securing their boards' commitment to spend a day together every year in a retreat setting, often discussing trends and identifying critical issues, as a tried-and-true way to break down barriers and reshape attitudes.

INSUFFICIENT GOVERNING KNOWLEDGE AND SKILLS

"Welcome to the Frontier" opens the section in chapter 1 that describes the state of the art in the rapidly evolving, still-developing field of public/nonprofit governing, which unlike more established fields lacks universal agreement on core principles and best practices. Around fifteen years ago, working on a book on nonprofit board leadership, I hired a research assistant to survey the governance literature over the prior decade and fill me in on major advances in both theory and practice so I could supplement what I'd learned from years of hands-on experience.

When Matilda reported her preliminary findings, she said she'd learned something that had amazed her: the lack of a detailed, comprehensive description of the work that boards actually do when they govern (as contrasted with such nongoverning work as raising money and making speeches). "So what are people saying governing is?" I asked. Her response: "Well, 'policy making' pretty well sums it up," she responded. Sad to say, hundreds of one-on-one interviews with board members since then have taught me that "policy making" remains the most common definition of governing work, followed by "oversight." Is it any wonder, then, that board members reach the boardroom without a nuts-and-bolts grasp of the work they're expected to do, and that many superintendents reach the top spot in their districts unprepared to play their role as the board's "chief governing partner" fully?

While the paucity of really detailed, nuts-and-bolts governing knowledge is an impediment to governing effectiveness and a solid board-superintendent partnership, education and training has proved to be an effective antidote. However, bad knowledge is harder to eradicate. In chapter 1 I talk about "insidious foes": erroneous assumptions about one or another aspect of the governing function that appear plausible and are often promoted by so-called governing gurus. Experience has taught that they can seriously impede governing performance and erode the board-CEO working relationship. You might recall the real-life case I share in chapter 1, about the damage that the erroneous assumption that policy making is the essence of governing can do. In that case, adhering to what is known as the "policy governance" approach meant that far too little attention was paid to steps aimed at keeping the board-superintendent working relationship healthy.

UNDERDEVELOPED SCHOOL BOARD COMPOSITION

A couple of months ago I sat in on a three-hour work session of the governance committee of the board of a nonprofit community and economic development corporation, refining a profile of attributes and qualifications the corporation should use in identifying candidates to fill upcoming vacancies on the board, for example: "successful experience on other nonprofit boards," "a passionate commitment to developing our community's economy," "a collaborative team player," "extensive connections with key stakeholders in our community," "willing and able to commit the time necessary to participate actively in governing," etc. The plan, which was subsequently executed, was to use the refined profile in recruiting candidates for open board seats. This is a common strategy in the nonprofit world for strengthening the board's governing capacity. It's straightforward and simple to implement, and I can attest to the positive impact it's had on the governing functions of hundreds of nonprofits.

By contrast, the open seats on the overwhelming majority of school boards are filled by election, which means school district executives and board members have no direct influence on their board's composition. The very sensible attitude is that we've got to work with the members the electorate sends, meaning that indirect strategies must be employed in developing a school board's composition. The most common strategy is to provide new board members with governance education and training, including attendance at state and national conference sessions focusing on governance, orientation of incoming board members, and learning through doing, principally by participation in board standing committees. Some districts—but not many, so far as I can tell—have attempted to indirectly influence the electorate as a way of building their boards' composition—by sending board members out to speak in forums such as chamber of commerce, Junior League, and Rotary luncheon meetings, telling audiences about the board's role and functions and the attributes and qualifications that make for effective board members.

THE CENTRIFUGAL FORCE AFFECTING THE BOARD

One of the reasons that it's so difficult to transform school boards into cohesive governing teams is the centrifugal force created by the election process. Many if not most newly elected board members, in my experience, arrive in the boardroom feeling conflicted. On the one hand, my interviews indicate they really are committed to student achievement as the preeminent bottom line of the district, and they sincerely want to work with their board colleagues in doing a credible job of governing. On the other hand, these newcomers to the board naturally feel loyal to the constituency that elected them. Sad to say, I've come across many instances where the centrifugal force created by constituent loyalty seriously dilutes board members' commitment to teamwork and conflicts with their governing responsibilities. I encountered a dramatic case of divided loyalty working against sound governance a few months ago: a new board member who voted against putting a sales tax increase on the ballot in the upcoming election even though she was convinced (so she testified in my interview with her) that her colleagues on the board had made a compelling case for the ballot issue. She just couldn't "betray" the anti-tax residents making up a large and highly vocal part of her constituency.

There's no way of totally eliminating the centrifugal force that the election process creates; that's a built-in, inevitable result of the way school board members are chosen. But there are practical ways of mitigating the forces that are discussed in the following chapters, including developing your board as a governing organization, making sure board members understand their governing role and functions, and engaging in team-building exercises.

THE ABSENCE OF BOARD ORGANIZATIONAL DEVELOPMENT

Finally, I frequently come across school boards that are seriously underdeveloped as governing organizations. Board members don't have a detailed understanding of their governing mission—the concrete governing work they've signed on to do, and these boards lack the structure (essentially standing committees) for channeling their governing work and the processes for engaging them in key governing areas such as strategic and operational planning. These underdeveloped governing organizations tend, unsurprisingly, to dramatically underperform, depriving their districts of the sorely needed leadership that these challenging times demand. *Board organizational development* isn't a widely used term at the present time, but of all the challenges to effective governance and a solid board-superintendent partnership, underdevelopment as a formal governing organization should probably top the list of barriers impeding high-impact governing.

THE KEYS TO OVERCOMING THE BARRIERS

The following eight chapters deal in detail with seven of the preeminent keys to a high-performing, high-impact school board and a close, positive, productive, and enduring board-superintendent working relationship:

1. A superintendent who is committed to playing the role of your district's chief governing partner: who is 100 percent committed to capitalizing on the board as a precious district asset and to working collaboratively with the board, who pays close attention to managing the relationship with the board, and who plays a leading role in developing the board's governing capacity.
2. Meticulous management of the board-superintendent working relationship: a close board chair-superintendent partnership;

clear board-superintendent communication and interaction guidelines; negotiation of superintendent-centric leadership targets; a well-designed process for board evaluation of superintendent performance.
3. Systematic development of the board as a governing organization: the key elements of board organizational development; ways to build an appetite among board members for board development; two major vehicles for updating the board as a governing organization: the governance retreat; and the governance task force.
4. Strengthened board self-management capacity: a clear board governing role and functions; systematic development of the board's composition and of board member governing knowledge and skills; management of the board's governing performance, including board self-assessment.
5. Well-developed governing architecture: the benefits of standing committees; the characteristics of a well-designed committee structure aligned with the board's governing functions rather than with operational and administrative "silos"; guidelines for ensuring that standing committees function as effective "governing engines."
6. Active, meaningful board member engagement in key governing processes aimed at producing effective decisions and judgments and fostering board member ownership: the role of standing committees in process design; engagement in strategic and operational planning; performance oversight; and external/stakeholder relations.
7. Strong executive support for the governing function: the formal, collective role of the executive managers as your district's Governance Coordinating Committee; the role of committee chief staff liaisons; steps to ensure full implementation of an updated board committee structure.

4

WHAT IS THE SUPERINTENDENT'S ROLE IN GOVERNING?

WELCOME TO THE C-SUITE

In my travels around the country, I see growing recognition that taking the helm as superintendent of a school district means joining a powerful profession: chief executive officer. Now the superintendent's peers and colleagues are other CEOs, not just of school districts but of all other public, nonprofit, and even for-profit organizations. By the way, since the traditional title "superintendent" does not sound very CEO-like to leaders outside the K–12 setting (after all, other "superintendents" manage coal mines and oversee utilities), readers will probably see it replaced over the years by more standard titles such as "chief executive officer" and "president and CEO." This likely development would certainly strengthen the superintendent's role in external/stakeholder relations, one of every CEO's top priorities.

Since the superintendent (CEO) position is different in kind from all other executive positions in your school district, newcomers to the C-suite are highly unlikely to have learned much about what's involved in being a full-fledged CEO in the process of climbing the district professional ladder. These newly minted CEOs are embarking on a radically new, extremely challenging, and often risky (a highly visible lightning rod for dissatisfaction that is dependent on an always-fragile relationship with the board) leg of their professional journey. Their long-term success depends heavily on aggressively seeking practical wisdom not only from other superintendents but also from the CEOs of other public and nonprofit sectors. For this reason, an increasing number of superintendents are regularly getting together in substate regions, often over lunch, to share notes on CEO-ship in their districts—especially how they're handling thorny issues reaching the C-suite, often relating to the board-superintendent partnership. And I'm seeing many superintendents these days become members of chamber of commerce and economic development corporation boards as an easy way to interact with CEO colleagues.

A HIGH-STAKES SUPERINTENDENT LEADERSHIP PORTFOLIO

As your district's chief executive officer, the superintendent is responsible for one of the highest priority CEO leadership portfolios—governance, which encompasses the governing work of your school board and the precious but always-fragile board-CEO working relationship (see chapter 5). In my experience, the superintendents who succeed in handling this highly complex, high-stakes portfolio have a couple of really important things in common. For one thing, they don't see themselves as simply the highest-ranking professional staff member reporting to their only boss, the school board. They know that this hierarchical we/they approach is doomed to failure.

They recognize that governing is a highly collaborative function shared by both board members and the CEO, and they understand that they're occupying a unique hybrid position: part top-ranking district executive/part district board member. In the for-profit sector, of course, the chief executive is virtually always a board member and often actually chairs the board. In the nonprofit sector, an increasing number of chief executives serve on their organization's board, typically as nonvoting board members, but in the public sector, including school districts, CEOs are never board members.

DE FACTO CAPTAIN

Another thing these successful K–12 chief executives have in common relative to the high-stakes governance portfolio they hold is a role I briefly touch on in chapter 2: de facto captain of your district's Strategic Governing Team: the school board, superintendent, and top administrators reporting to the superintendent. I can't overemphasize how critical playing this role fully is to a superintendent's long-run success. In a nutshell, as captain of the Strategic Governing Team, the superintendent takes accountability for your district board's effectiveness as a governing body, serving as the prime mover in developing the board's governing capacity, mapping out processes for board member engagement in governing processes, putting well-designed governing structure in place, and making sure the board-superintendent partnership is meticulously managed and remains healthy.

Now, as you'll see in the coming chapters, playing this role is a classic case of what we call "leading from behind." To take a practical example that I deal with in detail in chapter 6, as captain of the Strategic Governing Team, the superintendent must make sure that your board's governing capacity is systematically developed, but only the most foolhardy K–12 CEO would attempt to publicly lead and manage a board-development initiative. Rather, she would most likely convince the board president/chair to appoint a governance task force consisting of a small number of board members and the CEO herself, to come up with board capacity-building recommendations. But leading from behind doesn't mean the superintendent plays a passive role on the sidelines, feeding information to the task force, which converts it into recommendations. Rather, in addition to making sure the task force is well-supported, as captain of the Strategic Governing Team the superintendent would most likely take the lead in contracting with a professional facilitator for task force meetings and would participate actively in task force deliberations.

THE CAPTAIN'S MULTIPLE HATS

In his capacity as your district's Strategic Governing Team captain, the superintendent wears six "hats" that are described in detail in the following seven chapters, including:

- **Chief Governing Relationship Manager**: Making sure that the board-CEO partnership is healthy through clear communi-

cation/interaction guidelines, meticulous management of the board-superintendent and board chair-superintendent working relationships, and effective board evaluation of superintendent performance.
- **Chief Board Developer**: Building an appetite among board members for systematic development of the board's governing capacity, convincing the board president/chair to be a champion for board development, acquainting board members with vehicles for board development, playing a leading role in the board-development process.
- **Chief Governing Accountability Officer**: Making sure that your school board adopts a clear governing role and set of governing functions and that it has a well-developed self-management capacity, including systematically developing the board's composition and managing its governing performance.
- **Chief Board Architect**: Making sure that your board is assisted in carrying out its demanding governing functions by a well-designed structure of board standing committees serving as powerful "governing engines."
- **Chief Governing Process Designer**: Making sure that board members are true owners of their governing role and functions through active engagement in shaping governing decisions and judgments.
- **Chief Governing Enabler**: Making sure that the board is provided with the executive support required to function as a high-impact governing body.

SUCCEEDING AS STRATEGIC GOVERNING TEAM CAPTAIN

Wearing these six hats successfully depends on three primary factors, in my experience: the attitude the superintendent brings to her work with the board; the superintendent's commitment to playing the Strategic Governing Team captain role; and the superintendent's board-savviness. All three are critical to the superintendent's success on the governing front over the long run, but attitude is the preeminent factor in one important respect: approaching governing responsibilities with the wrong attitude virtually guarantees failure in dealing with the other two factors.

BRINGING THE RIGHT ATTITUDE TO THE GOVERNING GAME

I've become adept at telling pretty quickly whether a superintendent brings the kind of attitude to her work with the board that will enable her to succeed as captain of her district's Strategic Governing Team and as her board's chief governing partner. I always ask a superintendent I'm considering working with at our first meeting to tell me about his working relationship with the board. If I hear something along these lines, I can feel confident about our becoming partners on the governance front: "They're a great group of people—lots of talent, knowledge, experience, expertise—but, you know, I don't think they're coming close to realizing their potential as a governing body, and I really feel accountable for helping them get to the next level. I know they want to do a better job of governing, but they're just not sure how to go about doing it. I think we've got a pretty good working relationship, but I know it could be better, and I've got a gut sense that if we don't figure out how to get them more engaged in the governing process, it'll jeopardize our relationship."

By contrast, a few years ago I made a snap decision not to work with a superintendent whose response to my question was something like this: "As boards go, they're not all that bad. At least they know enough to stay out of my business, so I can't really complain about micromanagement. For example, they adopted next year's budget in a special board meeting a couple of weeks ago, and I'm pleased to report that it only took 35 minutes or so. Of course, we—the staff and I—had done a great job of putting the document together, so they couldn't easily quibble about it. That's what I really like in a board: let us do the detailed staff work, keep at a high level, and generally leave us alone to do our jobs. I'll make sure they get the information they need, when they need it, to make decisions, and it's their job to get the decisions made, not mine."

In my experience, truly board-savvy superintendents see their board as a precious district asset—perhaps the preeminent resource—and they feel strongly accountable for helping their board become a more effective governing body, and hence a more valuable asset. They really do believe in strong board leadership and want their board to get better at doing its governing work. I've never known a superintendent seriously aspiring to be a close governing partner with the board to bemoan the motley crew of board members she's been saddled with and express the heartfelt wish to contain the damage they might do if not closely watched. Well aware that the kind of people who get to the boardroom tend to bring good intentions with them, but also to jump in and fill vacuums wherever they find them, these superintendents ask how they can help their board members become fully engaged in doing really important governing work so that there's no vacuum to fill. I've also learned that superintendents who are seriously committed to partnering with their board don't think about the board in "we-they" terms. They know that they've got to be heavily involved in the governing process, functioning as a real governing partner with their board.

Nor do superintendents committed to strong board leadership and to a collaborative approach to governing sit around obsessing about the specter of micromanagement. On the contrary, they know that governing involves so much intensive board-staff interaction and collaboration that it doesn't make sense to waste time worrying about potential breaches in hard and fast boundaries; indeed, they don't see the boundaries as all that hard or fast. I'm reminded of a superintendent I worked with a few years ago who exemplified such nondefensive leadership in working with her board. I was sitting in on a special daylong work session involving the board, this superintendent, and her senior administrative team. The purpose was to review and assess progress in implementing a high-stakes change initiative the board had adopted a month earlier: opening a new magnet school for the arts. Shortly after our lunch break, we got involved a very detailed discussion about one of the major implementation challenges: recruiting qualified faculty willing to work at less-than-competitive salaries.

About thirty minutes into this very important and most interesting discussion, one of the board members, feeling guilty, said something like this: "I think we're getting into dangerous territory now. I know you all agree with me that the board should be primarily focused on what we do, not how we do it, and it seems to me that we're getting pretty deeply into the how. Maybe we should leave this to our superintendent and her staff."

Despite wearing my consultant hat, I kept quiet, curious how the superintendent—a very strong, self-confident executive with a commanding presence—would react. I couldn't have been more pleased when I heard her say she was quite comfortable with board members being involved in the discussion, since the stakes were tremendously high and she and her team needed board members' best thinking. Were board members actually getting involved in what might traditionally be considered administrative details? To an extent, perhaps. Did it bother the superintendent? Not a whit. Board members had valuable wisdom to share about a high-stakes matter, so why worry about a hypothetical barrier being breached?

MAKING GOVERNING A TOP-TIER SUPERINTENDENT PRIORITY

Every superintendent I've worked with over the years who has succeeded in playing the Strategic Governing Team captain role has treated governing as one of his top chief executive functions, typically along with strategic decision-making, financial resource development and external/stakeholder relations. In practical terms, this obviously means making a significant time commitment to working with the board—in my experience between 25 and 30 percent of a superintendent's time on the average. Where the time commitment is concerned, I strongly counsel rigorous self-auditing to make sure the time is actually being spent on governing matters since self-deception is always a clear and present danger. I've come across more than one superintendent over the years who's convinced himself that he's devoting significant time to governing when, in reality, he's put it lower on the list than CEO functions that feel more familiar, comfortable, and satisfying, such as strategic planning and financial management.

I worked closely on a couple of occasions with a woman who was in many ways a brilliant superintendent—visionary, extremely bright, highly innovative, and extraordinarily energetic. There's no question she believed in the importance of high-quality governing, as evidenced by her taking the lead in helping her board update its governing role and modernize its standing committee structure. But it turned out to be extremely difficult for her to devote sustained attention to the governing function, and as a result the new committee structure ended up being only tenuously established and consequently seriously underperforming. What really struck me was that she appeared genuinely unaware that governing was taking a back seat to priorities that titillated her executive palette.

It's also important to keep in mind that a superintendent's devoting at least 25 percent of his time to the governing function won't mean it's a top CEO priority in practice unless that time is thoughtfully allocated. Otherwise, it's all too easy for a superintendent to spend a disproportionate amount of his governing time doing what comes naturally or feels familiar and comfortable. A few years ago I worked with a superintendent who was a consummate people person who loved—and was very good at—schmoozing with board members. There's no question his interpersonal skills played an important part in building a positive working relationship with the board, and I've seen many a superintendent's cold and aloof style alienate board members. But, predictably, overreliance on schmoozing and inattention to such critical matters as figuring out how to engage the board meaningfully in strategic decision making eventually resulted in a parting of the ways between this affable superintendent and his board. By the way, I've seen just as many cases of superintendents whose inattention to the interpersonal dimension has eroded their working relationship with the board despite their mastery of the "harder" aspects of governing.

I've learned a very useful technique from superintendents who have employed it with great success behind the scenes: acting as the "executive director" of the governing "program," which encompasses the board, all of its governing processes, and the staff work involved in preparing for—and following up on—committee and full board meetings. Thinking of the governing function as a very important program that the superintendent is responsible for managing is a practical way of translating the priority into actual practice. One superintendent I know who makes effective use of this technique devotes a couple of hours every weekend to assessing "program" progress and doing "program" planning in two areas:

- Ongoing board operations: How is the governing process functioning? What issues have come up that need attention (e.g., lagging attendance at planning committee meetings or inadequate staff preparation for performance-monitoring committee meetings)? How should they be addressed (e.g., bringing the attendance issue up at the next governance committee meeting for discussion)? What major governing events are on the horizon that need special attention (e.g., the annual strategic planning work session, which needs to be on the agenda of the next executive team meeting to ensure adequate preparation)?
- Long-term board development: What serious long-term board-development issues are emerging, such as the need for an updated board role description, or an inadequate process for orienting new board members, which is resulting in board members who take an inordinate amount of time learning the governing ropes? What steps need to be taken to deal with the emerging issues, such as impaneling a governance task force or holding a special governance work session? What's the most effective way to bring these developmental issues to the board's attention, for example, jointly with the board president at the next governance committee meeting?

A REALLY BOARD-SAVVY SUPERINTENDENT

Every superintendent I've worked with over the years who has succeeding in the Strategic Governing Team captain has understood the governing business inside and out—the detailed nature of governing work, the architecture of the board in terms of its governing role and structure, and the processes for board engagement in key governing areas, such as planning and performance monitoring. As governing aficionados, they stay abreast of advances in the rapidly developing mother field of nonprofit/public governance—for example, the move away from traditional comprehensive long-range planning as a process for board involvement in strategic decision making, and the emergence of a leaner, more issue-focused approach to planning explicitly aimed at accomplishing strategic change. They're avid consumers of books and articles dealing with governance, and they seek out workshops offering nuts-and-bolts guidance on governance matters.

The compelling reason for a superintendent's becoming a world-class expert in governance is obvious: to be able to play the roles of chief board developer and chief governance process designer effectively. For example, if a superintendent isn't familiar with current thinking about board standing committees as a vehicle for getting the detailed work of governing accomplished, how can that superintendent help the board update or fine-tune its governing structure? Equally important, without a firm grasp of the rapidly evolving field of nonprofit and public governance, how could a superintendent help her board avoid taking steps that might actually work against high-impact governing? This is extremely important because, as I observed in chapter 1, the field of nonprofit/public governance involves much more art than science. The literature has been relatively scant until recently, and there still isn't a universally accepted body of governance principles and standards that boards and superintendents can follow. On the contrary, governing principles and methodologies are frequently hotly debated, and the number of what I call "fallacious little golden rules" that are floating around in the governance universe can easily lead unwary consumers, including superintendents, astray—all too often even jeopardizing their positions.

5

HOW CAN WE BUILD A SOLID BOARD-SUPERINTENDENT PARTNERSHIP?

A CAUTIONARY TRUE TALE

A few years ago, I walked into the office of a superintendent I'd known for a couple of years—an extremely bright and thoughtful chief executive officer who had over his two years at the helm of his southeastern district made tremendous progress on the administrative front, including bringing in two new department heads to fix serious deficiencies in the financial and human resource management areas. District educational performance was steadily improving, and he was immensely popular among the principals and faculty in the district's eight buildings. I was surprised to find my colleague slumped at his desk, head in hands, looking distraught. When I asked what had happened, he handed me a copy of the email he'd received earlier that morning from his board president, following up on an executive session of the board the night before to review the superintendent assessment questionnaires that all nine board members had completed. The bottom line: unanimous agreement that, while he was an exemplary educational and administrative leader, he'd badly dropped the ball in working with the board, whose members felt taken for granted and disrespected. They'd been caught off guard several times over the past two years by developments the superintendent hadn't briefed them on, and the regular quarterly one-on-

one meetings with the superintendent over breakfast or lunch they'd requested over and over again hadn't yet gotten off the ground.

Sad to say, this highly capable superintendent's partnership with the board was so badly frayed that it couldn't really be repaired, so at the end of his third year on the job, his contract wasn't renewed. The lesson? A superintendent who takes her eye off the board-relationship ball is playing with fire, professionally speaking. Over my quarter-century of work with boards and their chief executive officers, for every board-superintendent relationship I've seen fatally frayed because of a superintendent's substantive performance shortfalls, I've seen ten bite the dust because of the superintendent's mismanagement of the working relationship with the board. How to build and sustain a close, productive, and enduring board-superintendent partnership is what this chapter is all about. Let's begin with the factors that make relationship building a real challenge for superintendents.

RELATIONSHIP-BUILDING CHALLENGES

Keeping the board-superintendent working relationship on an even keel and healthy over the long run is a major challenge. Just the fact that strong-willed people with robust egos have to be melded into enough of a team to do the extremely complex and demanding work of governing is challenging enough, but other factors help to make the board-superintendent partnership inherently fragile and prone to erode quickly if not diligently managed. For one thing, the high-pressure atmosphere at the top of school districts, where high-stakes and often tremendously thorny issues are addressed—frequently with intense public scrutiny—tends to fray the board-superintendent partnership. And school board members, the great majority of whom are elected by residents of their districts, often feel more beholden to constituencies than to their board colleagues, and are notoriously difficult to meld into a cohesive governing team. And I've run into several school boards over the years whose members are significantly out-ranked—professionally and in terms of compensation—by the superintendent, often contributing to corrosive envy on the part of board members.

THE SUPERINTENDENT AS CHIEF GOVERNING RELATIONSHIP MANAGER

Superintendents who take the relationship with their school board seriously, making it a top CEO priority, well know that they've got no choice but to take the lead in meeting the board-superintendent relationship challenge. It might theoretically be a shared responsibility, but the reality is that being unpaid volunteers who have enough of a challenge mustering the time and energy to do a bang-up governing job, board members can't be expected to take the lead in managing the working relationship with their CEO. The great majority of school board members I've worked with over the years have recognized that keeping the relationship with their superintendent healthy is a high priority, and they've been willing to serve on a committee charged with overseeing and developing the partnership, but they typically expect the superintendent to wear the chief governing relationship manager hat.

To be sure, the average board member would probably lose some sleep over a souring relationship, knowing that it would negatively impact both governance and district educational performance. But they'd expect the superintendent to take the lead in figuring out exactly what the relationship problems are and to take the initiative in fixing them, and they'd be highly unlikely to blame themselves for a failed relationship. As really board-savvy superintendents well know, they're the ones who inevitably take the blame for relationship problems, and if the board-superintendent partnership breaks down completely, the board will fire the superintendent, not itself.

This chapter focuses on five critical relationship maintenance strategies that the board-savvy superintendent, in her capacity as chief governing relationship manager, can employ in collaboration with her board:

1. Formally, explicitly assign responsibility for overseeing and maintaining the board-superintendent partnership to a board standing committee—governance or board operations—headed by the board chair and consisting of the chairs of the other board standing committees and the superintendent.
2. Under the leadership of the governance or board operations committee, establish and implement detailed guidelines for

board-CEO and board-executive team communication and interaction.
3. Pay special attention to building strong working relationships between the board chair and superintendent and between each of the board's committee chairs and the superintendent.
4. Implement a well-designed process for regular, formal board evaluation of superintendent performance.
5. Employ extensive informal board-superintendent and board-executive team interaction as a bonding mechanism.

A BOARD HOME FOR RELATIONSHIP MANAGEMENT

Assigning responsibility for overseeing and managing the board-superintendent working relationship to a mainline board standing committee (see the detailed description of well-designed board standing committees in chapter 8) is perhaps the surest way to ensure that adequate attention is paid to the relationship and that potentially damaging relationship issues aren't allowed to fall through the cracks. And because the board operations or governance committee is typically headed by the board president/chair and consists of the chairs of the board's other standing committees (such as planning and performance monitoring) and sometimes other board officers, such as the board vice chair or treasurer, it is an ideal body to pay close attention to such a high-stakes, notoriously fragile relationship that can easily erode if not meticulously managed. Not only does the composition of the board operations or governance committee signal that the board-superintendent relationship is a high governing priority, but it also lends credibility to any agreements reached with the superintendent that normally require full board approval, such as the superintendent's annual leadership priorities and action to address a serious relationship issue.

Key responsibilities of the governance or board operations committee wearing its relationship management hat typically include:

- Establishing and periodically updating board-superintendent-senior administrator interaction and communication guidelines.

HOW CAN WE BUILD A SOLID BOARD-SUPERINTENDENT PARTNERSHIP?   45

- Ensuring that an effective process for evaluating superintendent performance is established and periodically updated, and overseeing the evaluation process.
- Annually negotiating superintendent leadership targets.
- And identifying and addressing relationship issues on an ad hoc basis.

INTERACTION AND COMMUNICATION GUIDELINES

Board-superintendent interaction became a major issue in a school district I worked with a few years ago. A new board member—let's call her Melinda—not long after her election began to visit elementary school buildings in the district, always arriving at the principal's office unannounced to chat about how things were going, what problems they were experiencing that she should know about, and how the board might help in solving them. Melinda also did some probing about the superintendent-principal working relationship, asking whether there were any issues she and her colleagues on the board should be aware of. Of course, the superintendent quickly heard about these visits, but he didn't want to do any red flagging without thinking the matter through. If he'd been tempted to wait, he was forced to act when he got a call one afternoon that Melinda had appeared in an elementary classroom that morning with no warning, sat in the back observing for a couple of hours, and stuck around until the lunch break to ask the teacher some questions about teaching methodology.

The superintendent understood that the unhealthy situation that'd developed in the district was due to the absence of guidelines to govern board member interaction and communication with the superintendent and senior administrators. He was board-savvy enough, fortunately, to recognize that he couldn't safely take on the job of disciplining an erring board member, and he needed to help his board assume the self-policing function. The solution? The school board president, having been briefed by the superintendent, called a special work session of the board's governance committee to flesh out a set of interaction and communication guidelines that were soon thereafter formally adopted by the school board. The interaction guidelines included this proviso: "School Board members are encouraged to visit school buildings in the district, but such visits shall be arranged through the Office of the Superintendent, which will ensure that such visits do not unduly inconvenience building administrators and faculty or disrupt classroom activities." Other guidelines relating to interaction included:

- "Only the board collectively may provide direction to the superintendent, and only to the superintendent."
- "Neither the board as a whole nor an individual board member may provide direction to any administrator under the superintendent."
- "Individual board members may request information from the superintendent or administrators reporting to the superintendent, provided that: the information is easily accessible and does not require more than a few minutes to obtain for the requesting board member; and the superintendent is formally notified by the board member requesting information from one of the superintendent's administrators and, via the superintendent, the full board."

While the board-superintendent (and staff) interaction guidelines on this list created boundaries that help to avert the development of issues that might erode the superintendent's working relationship with his board, the communication guidelines they developed were intended to serve as an adhesive, strengthening the board-superintendent bond and making it more resistant to erosion. For example:

- "The superintendent shall make sure that board members are never caught off guard and embarrassed publicly by important events they're unaware of."
- "The superintendent shall pay close attention to regular, formal communication with the board, via a bi-weekly e-update on major developments not only within the district but also at the state and national level and via the superintendent's report at monthly board meetings, making sure that board members are apprised of such superintendent activities as meetings with key stakeholders."
- "The superintendent should meet one-on-one with every board member at least quarterly to discuss issues of special interest to the board member."

BUILDING A SOLID BOARD PRESIDENT/CHAIR-SUPERINTENDENT PARTNERSHIP

Experience has taught that a superintendent's investing in the development of a rock-solid working relationship with her board president/chair can yield powerful organizational dividends. In fact, I would suggest that one of the preeminent priorities of a truly board-savvy superintendent is to transform her board president/chair into a strong governing partner, a reliable ally, and when needed, an ardent change champion. The board president/chair makes an especially important partner for the superintendent not only because of her formal authority as "CEO" of the governing board, but also the fact that board chairs are often major actors who wield tremendous influence in their communities. I've seen board-savvy superintendents successfully employ five major strategies in building close and productive working relationships with their board president/chair:

1. Reach agreement with the board president/chair on the fundamental division of labor with the superintendent.
2. Get to know the board president/chair really well.
3. Actively help the board president/chair succeed in her formal governing role.
4. Actively assist the board president/chair in having a richer, more satisfying experience beyond her formal leadership role.
5. Never miss an opportunity to provide the board president/chair with ego satisfaction, often in little but important ways.

DIVVYING UP THE LEADERSHIP LABOR

"I'm not sure why you're talking about superintendents reaching agreement with their board chairs on the division of labor. Isn't it pretty obvious?" My response to this question, which came up not long ago in a governance workshop I was conducting, was an emphatic "Yes and no." Yes, it's true that the board chair is the formal leader of board deliberations, and normally board bylaws specify that he has the authority to appoint the chairs and members of the board's standing committees and ad hoc task forces and committees and to refer matters to the appropriate committee. But when you think about it, even that seemingly clear responsibility must be shared with the superintendent for the simple reason that board chairs, being part-time volunteers for the most part, can't possibly play their board leader role alone. Active collaboration with, and strong support from, the superintendent is essential for their success. And in the realm of external relations, both the board chair and superintendent are commonly viewed as major actors, so they'd better pay some attention to coordination and division of labor or they'll be stumbling all over each other. So every really board-savvy superintendent I've ever worked with has made a point of sitting down with a new board chair to discuss in detail how they'll be working together.

GETTING TO KNOW THE BOARD PRESIDENT/CHAIR

Board-savvy superintendents who excel at partnering with their board chair always, in my experience, make a concerted effort to get to know their preeminent partner in-depth as quickly as they can, in terms of:

- The resources that the board chair brings to her leadership role, including skills, expertise, knowledge, external connections, reputation, to name some of the more important attributes. This is especially important in enlisting the board chair to provide leadership beyond merely chairing board meetings, since it would obviously be counterproductive to call on the board chair for leadership he isn't capable of providing. For example, a few years ago I worked with a board chair—a labor leader—who was a virtuoso at behind-the-scenes negotiation but terribly ineffectual as a public speaker—with his uninspiring monotone delivery and tendency to stumble over words. His board-savvy superintendent knew enough to call on him as a partner in negotiating privately with key stakeholders like the county executive, but to avoid having him represent the district as a speaker in key forums like the monthly chamber of commerce luncheon or on radio talk shows.
- The board chair's style of communicating. One of the less board-savvy superintendents I've ever worked with taught me a lesson about the price of failing to pay attention to his board chair's style

a few years ago. The superintendent was finding it extremely frustrating trying to work with his relatively new board chair, an extraordinarily successful entrepreneur who had built a highly profitable company from scratch over the past quarter-century, without the help of a college degree. Over and over again, the superintendent would send his chair a well-crafted briefing paper on an issue coming up at the next board meeting, explaining why he was taking a particular position, only to receive no response at all. Charged with the responsibility to find out what was going on, I scheduled lunch with the chair, who shared with me how puzzled he was that the superintendent was continually sending him long issue papers. He explained that he was actually pretty offended since anyone who took the trouble to get to know him would understand that he infinitely preferred a face-to-face sit-down over having to wade through a briefing paper. By the way, the problem did get worked out—by the superintendent's changing his style and meeting for lunch once a week with his board chair to go over major issues deserving the chair's attention.

- The board chair's aspirations and special interests. Really board-savvy superintendents also make an effort to understand their new chair's professional aspirations and even more personal special interests, since, as I'll discuss later, one important way to strengthen the working relationship with the chair is to help her have a richer, more rewarding experience that goes beyond the formal board chair role. For example, a superintendent learned that his board chair was passionate about community and economic development issues and hoped that his leadership of the district might earn him a seat at the community development table.

NONMONETARY COMPENSATION FOR THE BOARD CHAIR

Board chairs are overwhelmingly unpaid volunteers, so truly board-savvy superintendents are always on the lookout for nonmonetary compensation that will not only reward the board chair for her service but also help to cement the board chair-superintendent working relationship. The most obvious is for the superintendent to go out of her way to ensure that the chair succeeds in his formal governing role. For example, one superintendent I've worked with without fail spends at least an hour on the phone with his board chair before every meeting of the board's governance committee, which the chair heads, going over the agenda point by point, answering any questions the chair might have, thereby making sure the chair is well prepared to lead discussion.

Another superintendent, whose board participates in an annual daylong strategic planning work session, not only always makes sure that her board chair plays a leading role in developing the agenda but also prepares opening remarks for the chair to deliver and ensures that her chair is assigned to the breakout groups in which she is most interested. And in the external affairs arena, a superintendent I know provides meticulous support for his board chair's speaking engagements on behalf of the district, not only making sure the chair is armed with talking points and visual aids but also even providing an opportunity to rehearse whenever the chair thinks it will help.

ENRICHING THE CHAIR'S PROFESSIONAL EXPERIENCE

In my experience, many less board-savvy superintendents can easily miss the opportunity to cement the relationship with their board chair by helping her enrich her professional experience beyond the strict boundaries of her formal governing role. This is an important way the superintendent can say, through concrete action, "I really do care about the quality of your experience, and I'll do what I can to make it more interesting and rewarding, beyond helping you succeed in your governing role." Don't doubt for a minute that such attentiveness can be a powerful relationship builder. Earlier I mentioned the example of board chair who was passionately interested in the area of community and economic development. As it happened, when the superintendent was asked to fill a vacant seat on the board of the county economic development commission, he recommended that, instead, his board chair represent the district on the commission board. When I was discussing this with the board chair a couple of months later, he made clear that he deeply appreciated his superintendent's consideration, telling me that he was "bowled over" by the superintendent's gesture.

And a tremendously board-savvy superintendent I was working with, knowing that her board chair was very interested in climbing the volunteer ladder in the state school boards association and eventually in the national association, went way out of her way to help her chair realize this professional vision. For one thing, she spent a half-day with her chair one Saturday, helping her map out a strategy for rising through the volunteer ranks, including volunteering to serve on ad hoc committees and task forces. The superintendent even put together a proposal for her and her board chair to present a workshop at the next state association conference, highlighting the governance improvements that had been implemented on the chair's watch. Not only was her chair touched by the superintendent's caring so deeply about her professional aspirations, but also the opportunity to work closely together in planning and presenting the workshop further solidified the relationship.

EFFECTIVE BOARD EVALUATION OF SUPERINTENDENT PERFORMANCE

I was fortunate to have the opportunity to sit in on a fascinating, highly productive work session a few months ago that lasted a little over three hours. The governance committee of the school board was conducting the end-of-year evaluation of its fairly new superintendent's performance. The first hour of the session was devoted to discussing the superintendent's performance in terms of district-wide outcome targets that had been established for the year just ended in the annual operational planning/budget process. The discussion focused on such important educational and administrative performance measures as graduation and drop-out rates, test scores, disciplinary actions, and the like. Achieving targets was noted, but most of the discussion centered on targets that were not met. By the way, the superintendent had prepared for the session by putting together an explanation for the shortfalls in performance that she knew would be highlighted.

The final two-thirds of the session were devoted to the superintendent's "CEO-centric" outcome targets that had been negotiated with the governance committee a little over a year ago. These targeted outcomes, which were explicitly tied to the superintendent's chief executive leadership priorities and which involved significant superintendent time, fell into four main leadership categories:

- District educational development—for example, the superintendent had committed to the full implementation of a strategy to strengthen classroom teacher performance, using a major foundation grant to finance professional development initiatives.
- External/community relations—for example, the superintendent had committed to significantly strengthening the district's relationship with the chamber of commerce.
- Internal management—for example, the superintendent had committed to significantly upgrading the district's financial management capacity, including hiring a well-qualified chief financial officer and completing a major overhaul of the accounting system.
- Board of directors support—for example, the superintendent had committed to working closely with the governance committee in developing and implementing a comprehensive program to strengthen board member governing knowledge and skills, including a completely redesigned process for orienting new board members.

The superintendent had also prepared for the latter segment of the evaluation session by documenting progress in achieving her CEO-centric targets and explaining any performance problems she had encountered. What hit me in the face as I observed this lively session was how substantive the discussion was from beginning to end. By focusing on two tiers of outcomes, the board's governance committee got to the heart of the superintendent's performance and was able to deal with truly important performance issues.

Board-savvy superintendents do their utmost to make sure that a substantive, meaningful process for the board to evaluate their performance, like the one I've just described, is designed and fully implemented. Not only do they want to a process that is outcomes-focused and hence protects the best interests of the whole district, the board, and the superintendent, but they also recognize that a well-designed and executed evaluation process is a major tool for keeping the board-superintendent working relationship healthy. The example of a meaningful process that I've just described is dramatically different from the kinds of mechanistic, ritualistic, and pseudo-scientific "instruments" that I've seen many districts and other nonprofit and public organizations employ. I can't tell you how many questionnaires I've come across that boards have used to "scientifically" measure CEO performance in major functional areas. For example, board members are asked to assess how effective the superintendent is in representing her district in the external world or in providing the board with support, or in filling top positions—often on a scale of 1 to 5. Being disconnected from concrete targeted outcomes, these patently subjective opinion surveys obviously widely miss the mark and can end up doing more harm than good.

INFORMAL INTERACTION

I'll bring this chapter to a close with a very brief look at informal interaction as a relationship-building tool. A couple of hours before every quarterly board meeting, the board, superintendent, and executive team of a Midwestern district get together for an informal lunch. There's no formal agenda; the point isn't to prepare for the upcoming meeting. Instead, board and staff members sit together at five-person round tables (preassigning seats ensures a mix of board and staff members at each table). The only formal guidelines are that that board business not be discussed at the tables and that participants get to know each other better. An interesting twist is that participants are requested to take another look before every quarterly pre-board meeting lunch at the extensive board and executive team member biographical sketches, including personal information such as kids' names and ages, that are maintained, and regularly updated, in a special section of the district's website. In practice, this simple technique has proved to be an effective conversation booster. Other districts I've worked with have brought board and staff members together at holiday parties and summer picnics—often with their families, and, as I've mentioned earlier, many board-savvy superintendents make a point of regularly sitting down over breakfast or lunch with individual board members.

Informal board-staff interaction might appear to be a somewhat frivolous topic, at least by comparison with what's come before in this chapter, but board-savvy superintendents know that such interaction breeds familiarity, which tends to be a glue more strongly binding relationships. To be sure, it's not a major-league partnership-building strategy, but enough finer touches like the quarterly lunch I described above can make a difference, so my counsel to superintendents is to capitalize on opportunities for informal interaction, as an important means of promoting intimacy and narrowing emotional distance—in other words, of humanizing—and deepening—professional relationships. Not only does it facilitate cooperation and collaboration, but it also creates a kind of line of credit that can be drawn on when tackling the kind of complex, high-stakes, tension-inducing issues that not only are common at the top of a district but also can seriously tax the most solid relationships.

6

WHAT DOES THE SUPERINTENDENT DO AS CHIEF BOARD DEVELOPER?

SYSTEMATIC BOARD DEVELOPMENT IN ACTION

The inaugural meetings of the school board's new governance, planning, performance monitoring, and community relations committees went as well as could be expected for brand-new committees that were a dramatic departure from the traditional "silo" structure they replaced: human resources, finance, and curriculum and instruction. The design principle undergirding the new committees had been a staple of business management in the United States for over a century: that form should always follow function. Applying this powerful principle in the K–12 governance realm meant that the board's standing committees should mirror the broad streams of ongoing board governing decisions and judgments: the board's management of its own governing performance, strategic and operational planning, performance oversight, and external relations. By the way, as I'll discuss in chapter 8, application of this hallowed structural design principle in this particular district had to be tailored to a small five-person school board. In practice, this meant employing what I call a "virtual" committee structure: organizing a monthly board committee-of-the-whole work session divided into committee segments, each headed by a different board member, a halfway house that nonetheless generated many of the benefits of standalone committee meetings.

Six months after those inaugural meetings, the new virtual committee structure was delivering on its promise: generating higher-impact governing decisions and judgments while also actively engaging board members in shaping their decisions. Not only was the district benefiting from stronger governance, but also board members were feeling more satisfied that they were making an important difference in the district's affairs, and their relationship with the superintendent was consequently on a more solid footing. This was serious organizational development in action, going well beyond merely training board members on their governing role and functions. The new structure was the culmination of a six-month board development process led by a board task force that included a number of other action steps intended to enhance the board's performance, including upgrading the process for managing the board's governing work and strengthening the process for board evaluation of the superintendent's performance. And it owed much to the superintendent wearing one of her preeminent chief executive leadership hats that I'll describe in this chapter: chief board developer.

BOARD ORGANIZATIONAL DEVELOPMENT IN A NUTSHELL

One of the core concepts that I describe in chapter 1 is your district's "Strategic Governing Team": the school board, superintendent, and senior administrators, who must work closely together to ensure that their district is well-governed. One of the critical decisions that every Strategic Governing Team must make is whether to systematically develop the board as a governing organization or just to inherit yesterday's board. If you're reading this book, you've probably already bought into the idea of board development because you know your district's effectiveness—and especially your students' educational achievement—depend on strong governance, as I point out in chapter 2. As I also observe in chapter 2, the case for paying close attention to systematic board development is even more compelling because your district's image is affected by your board's credibility as a governing body, and the kind of satisfied board members serving on well-developed boards make for more reliable partners for the superintendent.

WHAT DOES THE SUPERINTENDENT DO AS CHIEF BOARD DEVELOPER? 57

I'll deal later in this chapter with practical ways to build your board members' appetite for systematic development of the board's governing capacity, but first we should define what board development involves. A good place to start is a reminder of a point I made in chapter 2: that your board is essentially an organization within the mother district organization, a formally established, permanent entity consisting of people working together through formal structure and process to carry out a common mission: to govern. Seen this way, the school board is not fundamentally different from other organizational entities in your district, such as your two high schools, the office of the superintendent, the district finance department, and so on. Since your board is a concrete organizational entity it can always be developed to make it more effective in carrying out its mission, in the board's case, of course, governing your district. The tried-and-true ways of developing your school board, and any other organization for that matter, include:

1. Clarifying your board's work: its mission, role, and functions.
2. Developing the people making up your board: both your board's composition and your board members' governing knowledge and skills.
3. Building your board's capacity to manage its governing performance.
4. Updating your board's governing structure and processes.
5. Building and maintaining a solid board-superintendent working relationship.

MAJOR GOVERNING TUNE-UP VERSUS CONTINUOUS GOVERNING IMPROVEMENT

Experience has taught me that every three to five years it makes sense to take a close look at your board as a governing organization, identifying opportunities to strengthen its people, role, structure, processes, and so on, capitalizing on significant advances in the rapidly developing field of public/nonprofit governance. The point is to make sure your board's governing capacity matches the demands of a highly complex, evolving environment. This kind of major board tune-up is likely to be a dramatic step forward if your board is one of those classic deferred maintenance cases.

Not long before beginning to write this book, I worked with a board that had not undertaken any kind of systematic capacity building for ten years. Consequentially, important governing decisions were not being made in a timely fashion, the board-superintendent working relationship had become dangerously frayed, the board's structure was badly outdated, board members were feeling increasingly dissatisfied and frustrated, and the board's credibility in the community was at an all-time low. Granted, this is an extreme case of deferred maintenance, but going more than five years without a major governing tune-up can be extremely risky. This chapter focuses on two vehicles that have been successfully employed in carrying out the major three- to five-year board tune-up: the governance improvement retreat and the governance improvement task force.

The second approach, which I'll examine in chapter 9, is what I call "continuous governing improvement." It involves employing well-designed board standing committees as very effective vehicles for updating the processes for engaging board members in the various governing functions. This approach to board development is appropriate for benign situations characterized by a generally effective board that's doing a good job of carrying out its governing mission and whose members are satisfied with their governing role and working together as a reasonably cohesive team, and by a pretty solid board-superintendent partnership. Major structural change clearly isn't called for; tweaking is the name of the game in this benign context. For example, your board's performance monitoring committee might in a half-day work session during the last quarter of your district's fiscal year review all reporting to the board and identify opportunities to strengthen specific reports in terms of both content and format and to upgrade the process of report review and analysis. Or your board's governance committee might in a similar work session update guidelines for board-superintendent communication and interaction and tweak the process for evaluating superintendent performance to make it a more powerful tool for strengthening the board-superintendent partnership.

BOARD-SPEARHEADED DEVELOPMENT NOT THE WAY TO GO

I've never seen a school board, or any other public/nonprofit board, successfully take the lead in developing itself as a governing organization. Not only are many board members naturally resistant to the change that systematic board capacity building more often than not entails, but they also typically have neither the time nor the experience and expertise to spearhead developing their board as a governing organization. And on the rare occasions when a board does take its own capacity building in hand, the results can be quite unfortunate, as I've observed on a number of occasions over the years. For example, a distraught superintendent called me a couple of years ago asking my advice on a situation he found himself caught in. His board president had appointed an ad hoc committee of four board members to identify ways to strengthen the board's performance. Although the board president had made him an ex officio member of the ad hoc committee, the superintendent, assuming board members should control the process, unwisely played a passive support role as the committee proceeded to come up with some truly counterproductive steps to bolster the board's leadership.

The most egregious error in judgment was to recommend that the board go through a lengthy and expensive "policy governance process," which down the pike several months later resulted in a bloated book of policies—essentially rules of the governing game that actually focused more on distinguishing between the board's and superintendent's sphere of action than on how these two preeminent governing partners should work together in getting good governing accomplished. Almost as bad, the ad hoc committee recommended that the board not have any standing committees, but, rather, should employ a continuously changing cast of ad hoc committees to address specific governing issues as they emerged. The predictable result: board member involvement in a somewhat random array of issues that didn't add up to stronger governing decisions over the long run. I could recount many other horror stories, but it should be obvious that board-led board development can be a slippery slope to governing futility, if not chaos.

THE SUPERINTENDENT AS CHIEF BOARD DEVELOPER

In my experience, successful board development depends on your superintendent playing the chief board developer role with gusto. Of course, to play this role successfully, the superintendent must be truly "board-savvy" in the sense of keeping up with developments in the rapidly evolving field of public/nonprofit governance. She must be a master of the governing art with a detailed understanding of the nuts-and-bolts work involved in governing, the structural configurations and processes that support effective governing decisions and judgments, and approaches to building board governing capacity that have been thoroughly tested and found effective in practice. Superintendents who aren't world-class experts in the governing business can all too easily steer their boards in the wrong direction in building the board's governing capacity.

I saw this happen recently when a superintendent, correctly urging her board to make setting district strategic directions a high governing priority, then proceeded to wrong-headedly get the board embroiled in an old-fashioned comprehensive long-range planning process that ended up wasting hours of board time and sacrificing God knows how many trees generating a mammoth tome that basically laid out what was already going on in the district and failed to identify any really significant innovation initiatives.

Playing the role of your district's chief board developer involves two basic steps: first, getting at least a majority of board members committed to developing the board's governing capacity, and, second, actively engaging board members in a formal capacity building process.

BUILDING COMMITMENT A DAUNTING CHALLENGE

Building board members' commitment to undertaking a systematic development effort can be a real challenge for a number of reasons. In the first place, board members are typically exceedingly busy volunteers who have enough trouble keeping up with their current governing responsibilities, much less tackling the complex job of strengthening their governing capacity. Just getting through the mounds of paper typically sent to board members and managing to make committee and full board meetings is challenge enough. The great majority of board members whom I have worked with over the years have been so mired down in the trench of governing that even finding enough time to recognize that they need to enhance their governing capacity is a notable accomplishment. If they feel overwhelmed keeping up with their governing work now, you can bet that they will not welcome the opportunity to spend concentrated time updating their governing role, structure, and processes in the interest of higher-impact governing, and in the backs of their minds will also be the possibility of the new model taking even more of their precious time than the current one demands.

You should also keep in mind that once many board members have learned the ropes of governing on particular boards, no matter how inadequate the governing structure and processes might be in terms of the resulting impacts and products or how boring and frustrating participating in governing the district might be at times, these board members are at least familiar with the ropes. If they have a high-enough pain threshold and have been around long enough, they are likely to have built influential roles for themselves on the "old" board, hence becoming the "old guard" that resists reform.

These governing veterans who have spent so much time and energy over the years learning how to "work the system" to get results (and ego satisfaction!) can be vociferous opponents of the board's tinkering with its current governing model. Whether they are consciously aware of their motivations or not, what they are actually saying—by their actions if not in words—is: "I've toiled in the vineyards for years, plowing through tons of paper, spending countless hours trying to figure out what I'm supposed to be doing and how to make these committees work. Finally, I've got it down. I'm really doing a good job and getting some recognition for it, and you come along saying we need to think about better ways of doing our jobs on the board. Not on your life!"

And you should never underestimate how powerful fear of change can be, even among the typically high-achieving, tenacious, and disciplined people who populate boards. Hundreds of board design efforts have taught me that many quite smart and ambitious people prefer the known, however unexciting and even unproductive it might be, to the unknown, with its new challenges that they might not be up to handling. More often than not in my experience, the fear is of failure—of being challenged and finding oneself humiliated by failure. What makes fear of being inadequate so insidious is it is often hidden from the fearful themselves, who are quite capable of coming up with conscious rationalizations to justify their opposition. One common manifestation is what I think of as "killing change with a thousand sensible questions," which hides fear of change under the guise of tenacious devil's advocacy expressed in endless what-if questions: "But if we no longer thumb through the finished budget as we have for the past sixty-five years, won't we risk losing control of the dollars?"

A strategy to secure the board's commitment to engage in strengthening its governing capacity must deal with these realities. Successful strategies that I am familiar with have involved two key elements: building a hard core of board development "champions;" and whetting board members' appetite for the capacity building process.

CREATING BOARD DEVELOPMENT CHAMPIONS

The dynamic duo of board chair and superintendent is a precondition for convincing the board to take a close look at developing its governing capacity, and adding other board members to the core of champions will only strengthen the case. The reason for board development champions on the board is simple: people tend to pay more attention to colleagues and peers than to administrators, much less outsiders, especially when they are being asked to do something that might take significant time and cause more than a little discomfort. No board-savvy superintendent or experienced consultant would ever agree to appear before a board to make a case for undertaking a capacity-building effort unless—and it is a big condition—the groundwork had been laid by these hard core advocates for change.

Your board president or chair is an obvious candidate for preeminent champion of a capacity-building effort, by virtue of the chair's role as "chief executive officer" of the board (but certainly not of the district, of course!), in this capacity formally responsible for leading the board in doing its governing work. A board-savvy superintendent should turn first to the chair, aiming to turn him or her into an ardent board capacity-building champion and, with the superintendent, co-leader of the capacity building process. If the board chair already conceives of his or her role as including the development of the board's governing capacity, then securing the commitment to play the leading role in updating the board's governing role and structure will be easier, but, in my experience, many board chairs have only the vaguest understanding of their role and have given little thought to board development.

So the superintendent will likely need to engage in educating the board chair on the chair's role and on the subject of board capacity building as a first step, after which the superintendent can concentrate on getting the chair to own the champion's role. In this regard, I have found that describing systematic development of the board as a governing body as the board chair's leadership "legacy," or "imprint," more often than not appeals to the typical chair's sincere desire to have a positive impact on the governing process.

The board chair, superintendent, and other board development champions can employ various devices to whet their colleagues' appetite for engaging in board capacity building. For example, pertinent books and articles that describe developments in the field of K–12 governance might be circulated, as a means to get board members thinking about governing as a serious subject and to recognize that boards can be consciously, systematically developed rather than merely inherited. A higher-impact approach is to provide opportunities for board members to participate in workshops that deal with capacity building approaches. AASA and NSBA conferences typically include one or more sessions on governance.

Although it may sound a bit trivial and more than a trifle manipulative, being positive and focusing on the concrete benefits resulting from systematic board capability building tends to be more of a magnet in attracting development champions than bringing the news to your board that, no matter how hard its members are working, it is badly underperforming as a governing body and needs to be fixed. I have never met a person who, after investing hundreds of hours in an endeavor, welcomed learning that he or she was not succeeding. Therefore, effective board development champions know enough to describe the process of updating their board's governing model as "getting more out of life as a board member," "taking a top-notch board to the natural next leadership level" "making a good board even better," and the like.

TWO POWERFUL TURNING-POINT VEHICLES FOR BOARD DEVELOPMENT

Let's say it's been seven years since your school board last took the time to examine itself closely as a governing organization and to come up with a number of important steps to deal with board governing performance issues. There are worrying symptoms that appear too dangerous to ignore, including an increasingly frayed board-superintendent working relationship, two seriously underperforming board committees, and a souring culture characterized by nasty bickering at board meetings. What to do? This chapter will conclude with an examination of two thoroughly tested vehicles that have proved very effective when much more than just tweaking governing processes is called for: the governance improvement retreat and the governance improvement task force. Both can yield a powerful return on the investment of time and energy if they are well-managed and supported, both require roughly the same level of investment in terms of time and money, and both involve the kind of in-depth engagement that fosters board members' commitment. However, they are very different in terms of structure and process in order to fit very different circumstances.

The governance retreat involves a daylong or one-and-a-half-day board-superintendent-senior administrative team work session, after which an action report consisting of concrete board capacity-building recommendations is presented to the board and executive team in a special work session. The retreat makes sense when intensive involvement of all board members from the very get-go is viewed as critical to eventual board adoption and implementation of the action recommendations. The governance task force involves a subset of board members (typically no more than a quarter of the board's membership) and the superintendent coming up with the action recommendations over a series of four to five task force work sessions and presenting them to the full board and senior administrative team in a special work session. The governance task force makes sense when there is no compelling need for all board members to be engaged from the beginning of the capacity-building process and/or it is not feasible to get all board members together for a retreat.

I can say with assurance that either the retreat or the task force will serve your district well as a board capacity-building vehicle if it is meticulously staffed and managed. Both involve intensive board member involvement, which is critical to generating the ownership that is necessary for implementation of action recommendations. I'll conclude this chapter by describing other keys to successfully employing both vehicles. What I am sure will not work and should be avoided like the plague is for the superintendent or a consultant retained by the superintendent to merely study a board's operations, come up with recommendations, and try to sell them to a board whose members haven't been intensively involved. Audiences for finished work tend to feel too little ownership to fuel action, as most of our readers have no doubt learned.

KEYS TO A SUCCESSFUL GOVERNANCE RETREAT

Experience has taught me that a district can ensure that a governance improvement retreat succeeds in generating sensible, practical, and affordable capacity building by:

- Creating an ad hoc Retreat Steering Committee headed by the board president/chair and consisting of two to three other board members and the superintendent—making sure that the committee is as diverse as feasible in terms of being representative of the board's composition and board members' viewpoints.
- Retaining a consultant/facilitator with substantial governance expertise and experience to provide high-level support.
- Having the consultant/facilitator develop—on the basis of interviews and review of governance documentation—a detailed retreat design consisting of specific retreat objectives, a description of the retreat structure (including detailed descriptions of the breakout groups that will be employed), and the blow-by-blow agenda and present the design to the steering committee.
- Ensuring that the retreat design includes several breakout group sessions led by board members to ensure active engagement—typically two to three groups meeting concurrently in each of two to three breakout group rounds (for a total of four to nine different breakout groups over the course of the day).

- Making sure the consultant/facilitator provides the board members who will be leading the breakout groups with a detailed orientation on their role and their groups' tasks so that they will succeed in leading their groups.
- Distributing the retreat design—in the form of a memorandum from the steering committee members and the consultant/facilitator—to all retreat participants at least a week in advance of the retreat.
- Preserving and transcribing the breakout group worksheets, which the consultant/facilitator should draw on in writing the action report following up on the retreat.
- Involving the steering committee in reviewing and finalizing the consultant/facilitator's action report draft, transmitting the action report to all retreat participants in the form of a memorandum for the steering committee and consultant/facilitator.
- Having steering committee members present the action report recommendations to retreat participants in a special work session and having participants formally approve the action recommendations, typically by adopting resolutions moved by the steering committee.

I have found that the peers-presenting-to-peers approach works extremely well in securing board approval for such board capacity-building recommendations as fashioning a board governing mission describing the board's detailed responsibilities and adopting an updated structure of board standing committees, a set of standing committee operating guidelines, an updated set of board member governing performance standards, and a new process for board evaluation of superintendent performance. However, be advised that meticulous preparation is critical to success, including developing PowerPoint slides for the presentation and making sure steering committee members participate in a rehearsal session prior to the formal presentation so that they are comfortable with the slides and have an opportunity to discuss how to address anticipated questions.

KEYS TO A SUCCESSFUL GOVERNANCE TASK FORCE

Your district can ensure the success of a governance task force by:

- Making sure a board officer—preferably the board chair—heads the task force and assembles a diverse group of task force members, including, if feasible, one of the vocal critics of board capacity building (who in my experience often become champions for the eventual action recommendations, rather than critics sniping from the sidelines).
- Providing the task force with a detailed charge from the chair, covering the desired outcomes (e.g., an action report consisting of detailed recommendations for strengthening the board's governing capacity) and the process that will be employed (e.g., six work sessions over the next four months—three in person and three via teleconference).
- Engaging a consultant with substantial governance expertise and experience to prepare agendas and documentation for task force meetings, drawing on interviews and review of pertinent documentation, to facilitate task force work sessions, and to develop the action recommendations and write the action report.
- Engaging all task force members in presenting their action recommendations in a special work session involving the full board and executive team, employing PowerPoint slides.
- Holding at least one task force rehearsal to go over the slides and discuss answers to questions that might come up.

7

HOW CAN WE STRENGTHEN OUR BOARD'S SELF-MANAGEMENT CAPABILITY?

THE IMPOSSIBLE DREAM?

You'll recall that chapter 3 asks the question, "What can stand in the way of high-impact governing?" My answer includes the "centrifugal force" resulting from the process of filling board vacancies. Elected school board members arrive in district boardrooms around the country feeling understandably conflicted. On the one hand, they naturally feel loyal to the constituency whose votes won them a seat on the school board, and so far as I can tell they really do want to do a good job of representing this constituency, diligently addressing the issues they think are uppermost in the minds of their supporters. They have campaign pledges to make good on, and there's nothing wrong with that; after all, representing voters is a core principle of our democracy. On the other hand, based on hundreds of one-on-one interviews with school board members and the comments board members have made in NSBA and state school board association workshops I've conducted over the years, I'm confident that the great majority of school board members have the best interests of their district at heart. They're passionately committed to public education and particularly to fostering student achievement.

So we have an inbuilt conflict that without question makes building a cohesive governing team in the boardroom a tremendous challenge and militates against building your board's self-management capacity. The barrier appears so high and the odds so daunting that I venture to say that the great majority of Strategic Governing Teams don't even tackle board self-management. Why tilt at windmills with so much other important work to do? My one-on-one interviews over the years bear this out. I always ask the question, "How is your board engaged in managing its governing performance?" The answer I typically hear goes like this: "That's interesting; I've never given it much thought. I guess we're not doing anything, at least nothing I'm aware of." And when I raise the same question in workshops, the response is typically quizzical looks, raised eyebrows, and rolling eyeballs.

That's the bad news. But on the positive side of the ledger, experience has taught me two things. First, puzzlement can't be equated with serious resistance. I've learned that there's not really engrained opposition to the abstract idea of strengthening the board's management of its governing performance. The people who are elected to serve on school boards tend to be bright, high-achieving people who believe in accountability and sincerely want to do a credible job. They aren't at all opposed to being held accountable for their work in the boardroom; they just doubt that there's any practical way of building their boards' capacity to manage itself. Second, I have never encountered serious resistance—and I mean not once in thirty years—among board members to taking concrete steps to strengthen the board's management of itself as a governing body, once board members understand what's involved. When they clearly see the way to greater governing accountability, the will to travel the self-management road is inevitably there.

This chapter describes practical, affordable, and thoroughly tested steps your district's Strategic Governing Team can take to build the board's self-management capacity. Before getting into the nuts-and-bolts details, let's take a general look at what board self-management is all about and why making it a board development priority makes good sense.

BOARD SELF-MANAGEMENT IN A NUTSHELL

Developing your school board's self-management capacity involves moving on two fronts: developing your board as a human resource and developing the capacity to manage your board's governing performance. Board human resource development deals with two major questions. First, how can we shape our board's composition? Second, how can we strengthen board members' governing knowledge and skills? Board performance management deals with three major questions. First, what performance targets should our board as a whole and individual board members hold ourselves accountable for? Second, how can we monitor governing performance? And third, how can we realistically deal with performance shortfalls?

On the board human resource development front, the default answer to the question about shaping our board's composition is simple: We can't! Our board members are elected, we can't get involved in local politics, so our hands are tied. End of story. Well, there are practical ways a district Strategic Governing Team can enrich the composition of the school board without venturing onto dangerous political turf, but they are indirect and unpolitical, as I'll discuss later in this chapter. I submit that any member of your district's Strategic Governing Team who is seriously committed to high-impact governing can't avoid dealing with board composition for the simple reason that the attributes and qualifications of the people serving on your school board have a huge impact on governing decisions and judgments. Once people have arrived in the boardroom, we can make sure that they hit the ground running by providing them with a thorough orientation on their governing roles, and responsibilities and on the structure and processes that have been put in place to help them govern effectively. And, of course, we can make sure their governing knowledge and skills are regularly and systematically updated.

Governing performance management deals with multiple performance levels: the board as a whole, the board's standing committees, and individual board members. Handling this facet of board self-management well depends on putting in place structure to house the performance management function so it doesn't ooze away like a crustacean without a shell, identifying reasonably concrete and objectives targets, making sure performance is monitored, and taking appropriate action in the case of performance shortfalls, such as tweaking board governing structure and processes and providing focused education and training. One of the challenges in this area is to avoid gimmicky, highly subjective individual board member self-assessment questionnaires, which have proved to be a weak tool for strengthening performance, as I'll discuss below.

IT'S WELL WORTH TACKLING BOARD SELF-MANAGEMENT CAPACITY

Experience has taught that your district will reap a rich return on its investment in building your school board's self-management capacity. Most importantly, traveling the self-management road fosters an accountability culture on the board that inevitably boosts governing effectiveness. The ultimate beneficiaries of stronger governing performance are obviously our district's preeminent "customers," the students whose educational achievement is bolstered because board members take their governing responsibilities seriously. The return on your district's investment in strengthening board accountability includes three less obvious but important benefits: strengthening your district's image and credibility, building a more cohesive board governing team, and relieving your superintendent of the need to serve as a kind of board disciplinarian.

If your district's board members and superintendent make an effort to brief the community on the board's progress on the accountability front—principally by speaking in public forums—taxpayers tend to take a more positive view of the district, in my experience. They feel more confident that their tax dollars are being put to good use as a result of a self-managing board that takes accountability for its governing performance. In these days of widespread public skepticism and distrust of institutions generally, and especially of governmental and quasi-governmental organizations, an improved public image is literally money in the bank for a school district relying on voter-approved tax financing. And, by the way, a board popularly viewed as an accountable governing body tends to be a magnet for potential school board candidates, since high-achieving people want to know that their governing work will be worth their time.

Some readers might think that school board members are likely to resist having their governing work monitored and measured, but the opposite is true. The kind of high-achieving, well-intended volunteers populating school boards got where they are professionally by setting and hitting targets. They want to be part of a top-notch governing board they can take pride in, and so they naturally welcome having their governing work assessed. And, by the way, the enhanced esprit de corps fosters a more cohesive governing team better able to carry out its governing mission in a collegial fashion. And when board members are actively managing their own governing performance, superintendents don't have to erode their chief executive line of credit by pressuring board members to do their governing job thoroughly. In my experience, while occasional superintendent prodding might make sense (especially if it's couched as encouragement), the need lessens considerably when a board has taken its own performance in hand.

A BOARD OVERSIGHT COMMITTEE

Since board members and superintendents are extraordinarily busy people, if a major governing function doesn't have a formal organizational home, the likelihood of its being accomplished fully in a timely fashion is slim. This is especially true when the function is as complex and against the grain as board self-management, which, as our readers know, tends to be a notable exception to the rule in the realm of K–12 governance. Your board's governance or board operations committee (see chapter 8)—typically headed by the board president/chair and consisting of the other standing committee chairs and the superintendent—is an excellent choice to house board accountability, in light of its essentially serving as a committee on board affairs. And the fact that standing committees, as I'll discuss in detail in chapter 8, are true "governing engines" that do much of the detailed work of governing argues for an oversight committee consisting of other committee chairs.

In order to carry out its role as the overseer of the board self-management functions, the governance or board operations committee must, first, make sure that these functions don't get lost in a pile of other responsibilities, as can all too easily happen. The solution is relatively simple: first, making sure that the formal goals statement of the governance committee includes responsibility for overseeing specific board self-management activities; second, ensuring that ongoing monitoring processes are spelled out in detail; and, third, formally incorporating board self-management activities in the governance committee's detailed annual workplan. The committee's annual workplan would, for example, specify precisely when during the upcoming fiscal year the committee would be updating/fine-tuning the board's governing mission and the board members' governing targets and standards, and when the committee would hold its annual board performance assessment work session.

DEVELOPING YOUR BOARD'S COMPOSITION

A governing board isn't an abstract organizational unit within the mother organization; it's essentially living and breathing human beings. And the people serving on the board, more than any other factor, determine how effective the board will be in carrying out its governing responsibilities. Recognizing this, many—probably the great majority of—nonprofit boards, which are overwhelmingly self-appointing, devote substantial time every year—typically through the board's governance or board operations committee—to filling vacant board seats with qualified candidates. Their governance committee develops a detail profile of desired attributes and qualifications to use in identifying and screening candidates to fill board vacancies: for example, having successful experience on other nonprofit boards, being committed to the nonprofit's mission, being able and willing to commit the time to participate fully in the deliberations of the board and the assigned standing committee, being a collegial-style/team player, having a high community profile, having extensive community connections, and the like. And many boards take this a step further by pinpointing particular sectors and groups that should be represented on the board (e.g., small business, CEOs, women, racial minorities, etc.).

This obviously isn't in the cards in the K–12 sector, where almost all school board members are elected. But a growing number of school boards around the country, recognizing the people serving on school boards have a tremendous impact on governing effectiveness, are exercising indirect influence on their composition. The process typically begins by the board's governance or board operations committee (see chapter 8) updating a profile of desirable board member attributes and qualifications and, after securing full board signoff, sharing the profile in a wide variety of community forums, such as chamber of commerce and Rotary luncheons and civic association meetings. The point is not only to raise public consciousness about the hugely important work school boards do and the board member traits that tend to strengthen a board's governing performance, but also to spark interest in running for the school board. I have no idea what difference these efforts are making in terms of strengthening school board composition around the country, but the high stakes involved certainly justify the effort.

CONTINUOUS DEVELOPMENT OF BOARD MEMBERS' GOVERNING KNOWLEDGE AND SKILLS

Governing is an urgent business in the K–12 sector, which is grappling with a constantly changing array of complex issues and a tremendously challenging environment characterized by strong voter resistance to tax increases, shifting federal and state priorities, and the like. School boards just plain can't rely on the old-fashioned spend-a-year-learning-the-ropes approach to integrating new board members into the board's governing processes. Getting up to speed as a new board member and remaining on top of the governing game depends on a continuous governing knowledge and skills improvement process spearheaded by the board's governance or board operations committee (see chapter 8). The first step is for the governance or board operations committee to annually update and formally adopt what you might call a "Governing Knowledge and Skills Improvement Program." This program would consist of two key components: orientation of new board members and continuing education for board members. The goals, operational content, and budget making up this Governance Knowledge and Skills Improvement Program should be annually updated by the committee.

I'll begin with the on-boarding process for new board members. In the "old days," orientation of new school board members was usually a job for the superintendent and her top administrators and was, ironically, focused heavily—indeed almost exclusively—on district operations: the educational services being provided, the revenue streams and budget, the missions and functions of key organizational units, and so on. This is ironic, because the focus on running the district rather than governing it makes the best of sense for new executives and managers, but doesn't come close to providing new board members with the information they need to participate in the governing process. The traditional focus was also ironic because it virtually invited board members to become immersed in operational details: ideal preparation for micromanagement!

In recent years, a new breed of board members and superintendents have transformed the orientation process, turning it into serious preparation for the actual role board members will be playing: governing the district. Key elements of this far-more-meaningful process include:

- Formal, annual governance committee adoption of an updated new board member orientation design developed by the superintendent, including the orientation structure (schedule of orientation sessions, presenter roles—who will be presenting what, presentation modes—such as use of PowerPoint slides, location, etc.), and orientation content.
- Heavy orientation program focusing on the governing function.
- Engagement of governance or board operations committee members in presenting the governing segment of the orientation program.
- Inclusion of a mentoring component in the orientation program.

Items typically covered in the governing component of the orientation program and backed up by documentation in a three-ring binder include the current board roster, including board members' professional and personal biographies; board policies; the board governing mission statement, outlining the board's major governing responsibilities; the current governing performance targets for the board as a whole, its committees, and individual board members; the standing committee structure, with a detailed description of each committee's functions; and guidelines for full board and standing committee operations.

Many school boards have found that mentoring is a powerful way to help new board members find their sea legs and to become productive members of the Strategic Governing Team. The concept is simple to implement. An incoming board member is assigned for four to six months to a more senior member who has spent at least two years on the board mastering the details of governing. The mentor might play an active role in the orientation process, as well as regularly meeting with the new board member to discuss issues and problems. The mentor might also assist the newcomer in negotiating the interpersonal relations terrain, helping her to understand the board's culture and to work through any interpersonal problems that might come up. There is also the team-building dimension of mentoring, which by making personal connections lessens the distance between newcomers and old hands and hence contributes to a more cohesive board culture.

The continuing education component of the governance committee's Governance Knowledge and Skills Improvement Program is intended to sharpen board members' governing skills and update their knowledge about advances in the rapidly changing field of K–12 governance. This component typically includes such elements as: a library of governing books and articles that are circulated among board members; on-site workshops dealing with particular facets of governance (e.g., new approaches for engaging board members in the innovation process or in annual budget development); rotating board member attendance at regional and national conferences with significant governance content, such as the AASA and NSBA annual conferences; and an annual daylong governance work session involving all board members, the superintendent, and senior administrators, for the purpose of fine-tuning the board's role, structure, and processes.

SETTING GOVERNING PERFORMANCE TARGETS AND STANDARDS

The governance or board operations committees of school boards around the country are developing targets and standards in the following board performance areas:

- Individual board member performance.
- Performance related to the whole board's handling of critical ongoing governing functions.
- Performance related to board culture (the rules governing board members' interaction with each other).
- Performance related to board capacity building.
- Performance related to standing committee operations.

If your board is committed to managing its own performance but has not developed any standards or targets, a good way to kick-start the process is for the full board, superintendent, and top administrators to spend a day together in a retreat setting, hammering out targets in the above areas (with the exception of standing committee performance, which should be measured against committee-determined targets). The board's governance committee can subsequently refine the targets and submit them to the full board for final adoption early in the fiscal year.

INDIVIDUAL BOARD MEMBER TARGETS AND STANDARDS

School boards that I've worked with and observed over the years have adopted such individual board member performance targets and standards as:

- Missing no more than one of the monthly board meetings in a given year or one of the standing committee meetings.
- Speaking on behalf of the district in specific public forums at least once a quarter.
- Being prepared for committee and board meetings.
- Participating actively in committee affairs.
- Participating in one governing skills development program annually.
- Representing the board at a minimum number of internal special events, such as graduations and employee recognition luncheons.

BOARD TARGETS AND STANDARDS

Board performance targets relate to your board's handling ongoing governing functions, such as:

- Regarding superintendent evaluation:

    1. The governance committee reaches agreement with the superintendent on a detailed set of superintendent performance targets at the beginning of the fiscal year.
    2. The governance committee formally evaluates the superintendent against these targets in a session with other board members and the superintendent present.

3. The governance committee and superintendent reach agreement on corrective actions the superintendent will take to address performance shortfalls. And so on.

- Regarding the board's role in strategic planning:

  1. The planning and development committee will host an annual daylong board-superintendent-senior administrator strategic work session at which the district's values and vision statements will be updated, environmental trends and conditions will be assessed, strategic issues will be identified and fleshed out, and strategies to address the issues will be brainstormed.
  2. The issues will be fine-tuned by the superintendent and senior administrative team and finalized by the planning and development committee.
  3. The planning and development committee will oversee task forces that will be established to fashion strategic initiatives to address the issues. And so on.

Your board's culture fundamentally relates to the norms that govern board members' interactions in board meetings and what participating in board meetings should feel like. For example, boards that I have worked with have established such standards as the following:

- Everyone will be encouraged to participate actively and to share their viewpoints.
- Board members will treat each other with respect and consideration.
- Board members will listen to each other's opinions, allowing them to be fully expressed.
- Board members will not bring hidden agendas to meetings.
- No board member will cut another down publicly.
- When the board has voted on an issue, board members in the minority will cooperate in seeing that the approved action is carried out and will not engage in back biting.

Capacity-building targets relate to actions that a board has agreed to take during the coming year to strengthen its governing structure and process, such as:

- Adopting a formal governing mission describing the board's primary governing responsibilities.
- Developing a profile of desired board member attributes and qualifications, to be employed in educating the public.
- Implementing a new standing committee structure.
- Holding the first board-staff prebudget operational planning work session.

BOARD STANDING COMMITTEE TARGETS

Standing committee targets relate to handling ongoing functions (e.g., the performance oversight and monitoring committee reviewing financial reports, identifying financial issues, and reporting the issues at the regular board business meeting) and to specific initiatives that particular committees have decided to tackle, above and beyond handling their ongoing functions: for example, the planning and development committee's deciding to radically redesign the annual retreat or to spearhead a visioning process involving extensive community participation, and the performance oversight and monitoring committee's deciding to work closely with the chief financial officer in moving to a new financial reporting format that will utilize creative graphics and for the first time report expenditures by major cost center.

RIGOROUS MONITORING AND PERFORMANCE ASSESSMENT

The only reason to invest in a formal board performance-management process is to improve board performance. In this regard, experience has taught me that the battle has basically been won when the targets and standards have been set. Board members are generally the kind of people who respond very affirmatively to target setting (after all, achieving targets is how they got where they are in life), making the performance targets virtually self-fulfilling. However, in order to ensure that questions regarding board performance are examined in the depth that they deserve, it is important that the governance committee set aside at least a half-day annually to assess the board's collective performance against the targets that have been set. The collective assessment should be reviewed with the full board in a work session (perhaps the second day of the annual strategic planning retreat), along with the governance committee's recommendations for remedial action, which will result in new capacity-building targets for the coming year.

Individual board member performance is a more sensitive area that demands a more nuanced approach. The boards that have handled this dimension of performance management most effectively have treated it as an ongoing monitoring process handled by the governance committee. Their focus is on board member growth and development, rather than blame and punishment. When performance shortfalls have been identified (say, a board member's missing two consecutive committee meetings, or frequently raising questions that were covered in written information sent to the board), they are typically dealt with through counseling and mentoring, which more often than not solves the problem.

8

HOW CAN WE MAKE USE OF BOARD STANDING COMMITTEES AS POWERFUL GOVERNING ENGINES?

THOSE POWERFUL GOVERNING ENGINES IN ACTION

I saw standing committees at work once again—for the umpteenth time—in a recent school board meeting, serving as the engines that drive every really high-impact governing board I've observed over the years. The chair of the board's strategic and operational planning committee, following up on a board-superintendent-senior administrative team strategic planning work session three months earlier, went through three strategic planning products, answering board members' questions. There weren't many questions about two of the products—updated district values and vision statements—since they'd been discussed in detail at the earlier work session. The third product, descriptions of three "innovation initiatives" to be fleshed out over the next couple of months, attracted most of the questions. One in particular—to develop in partnership with the local community college and chamber of commerce—was a nonprofit manufacturing skills training "academy." The strategic and operational planning committee chair also presented the preliminary agenda for the board-superintendent-senior administrative team prebudget operational issues work session kicking off the budget-preparation process that was scheduled the next month before passing the baton to the chair of the board's performance oversight and monitoring committee.

The performance oversight and monitoring committee chair first went through the quarterly financial report, employing the newly designed format—bar charts on PowerPoint slides comparing actual versus budgeted expenditures by major district cost centers. The chair spent a few minutes explaining a couple of issues the committee had red-flagged, involving late payments from a foundation funding a districtwide instructional improvement initiative and the need to fix a serious glitch in the upgraded accounting software that'd recently been installed. The chair then turned to the quarterly educational performance report, spending the bulk of her time discussing significantly lagging performance at the middle school. The district's chief financial officer/treasurer, sitting next to the committee chair, fielded a couple of questions the committee chair had tossed his way, but for the most part the chair ran with the ball, answering the great majority of board members' questions.

I was impressed, as I've been on many other occasions in other school board meetings, by the strong role the committee chairs played in the board meeting; they were clearly well-prepared and in command of their subject matter, and they very capably led discussion. And I was struck by how different this board meeting was from the traditional passive-reactive, staff-driven board meetings I'd observed over the years with board members, wearing their time-honored audience hats, mainly listening while staff talked—and talked, and talked, occasionally thumbing through documentation. How refreshing it was to see committee chairs play such an active leadership role, peers presenting to their peers. The energy in the boardroom was palpable.

GOVERNING CLYDESDALES AS WELL

When I first began working with public and nonprofit boards and their chief executives over thirty years ago, I wouldn't have made board committees a top-ten professional concern. Oh, I knew from my graduate work in management—particularly from reading Alfred D. Chandler Jr.'s path-breaking *Strategy and Structure*—that organizational structure is a key element in successfully translating mission and strategy into concrete practice, but I didn't really see it as a hugely important piece of the governance puzzle. After all, committees aren't a very scintillating or theoretically interesting subject. How wrong I was! It didn't take me long to realize that committees are one of the two or three most important factors determining the effectiveness of public and nonprofit governing boards. I don't mean just any committees, but well-designed ones. Later in this chapter I'll describe what a well-designed committee looks like and explain why poorly designed "silo" committees are infinitely worse than having no committees at all. For now, I'll focus on the value committees, if they are properly designed, can add to the governing process.

As the title of this chapter indicates, you can think of board standing committees as a kind of engine that drives the process of making governing decisions and judgments. The most obvious and visible benefit is extraordinarily important: committees do the indispensable preparation for board business meetings that leads to well-made governing decisions and judgments. Much of their preparation involves separating the wheat from the chaff so that board meetings can home in on the critical decision elements. Their pre-work directly leads to productive board meetings that might otherwise continue into the wee hours, wasting precious time and energy. Indeed, committees are powerful governing engines, but you can also think of them as like those majestic draft horses, the Clydesdales, pulling the Budweiser wagon in commercials: their broad backs are capable of carrying a huge load of precious cargo. In addition to serving as the drivers of productive board meetings, well-designed committees also:

- Turn board members into real nuts-and-bolts experts in the complex field of public and nonprofit governance and satisfied owners of governance decisions and judgments through in-depth participation in committee deliberations. While governing expertise obviously makes for more effective governing decisions and judgments, satisfied owners of their governing work also make for more reliable partners for the superintendent.
- Turn committee chairs into allies and change champions for the superintendent. Showcasing the chairs in public board meetings provides them with nonmonetary compensation in the form of ego satisfaction, and having committee chairs present all briefings and action recommendations in full board meetings turns the chairs into superintendent change champions and spear carriers

so that the superintendent doesn't have to expend finite and precious psychic capital convincing the board to act.
- Provide a forum for the superintendent and her top administrators to collaborate with committee members in developing processes for engaging board members in key governing functions such as strategic planning and performance monitoring. I'll get into this in real detail in chapter 9, which describes the process-design role of committees.
- Provide an opportunity for intensive board member interaction with the superintendent and senior administrators at an appropriate level. This results in the kind of bonding that contributes to a more cohesive and collaborative Strategic Governing Team.
- Foster trust among board members—and consequently a more cohesive board culture—through committee reports to the full board that keep all board members apprised of the deliberations taking place in committee meetings.
- Help keep board members out of the weeds of micromanagement. Well-designed standing committees keep their members focused at a high level on true governing issues, rather than on managerial and administrative details best dealt with by the superintendent and administrative staff.

WHAT A WELL-DESIGNED COMMITTEE LOOKS LIKE

Two of the classic organizational design rules that played a huge role in America's becoming an industrial powerhouse and generator of tremendous wealth in the twentieth century are that form should follow function and the closely related maxim that structure should follow strategy. The same basic organizational design principles apply to the standing committee structure of a public school district. You'll recall that in chapter 2 I defined *governing* as making judgments and decisions that flow along three broad functional streams: planning, performance monitoring, and external/stakeholder relations. Following the form-follows-function principle, then, we will want our committee structure to mirror these broad governing functions. Since the board's oversight and management of its own governing activities is also an important stream, a committee corresponding to this function also makes sense. And the audit function, which has become highly visible in recent years and is often explicitly mandated for public boards by state law, can be considered part of the performance monitoring stream, but is sometimes handled by a standalone committee.

Figure 8.1 depicts a model committee structure embodying the form-follows-function design principle. Before I describe the primary functions of these four model committees, which are being employed by a rapidly growing number of public and nonprofit boards around the country, including school boards, I'd like to venture briefly into the dark side of governance: silo committees.

THOSE DASTARDLY, DEADLY SILO COMMITTEES

Experience has taught that traditional "silo" committees are a slippery slope to board underperformance and the erosion of the board-superintendent partnership. A so-called "silo" committee reflects your district's administrative and operational structure, rather than the broad governing functions embodied in the model structure we just described. Typical silo committees, which you can think of as tips of the administrative and operational icebergs, include curriculum and instruction, pupil services, buildings and grounds, personnel or human resources, finance, and the like. These narrowly focused committees that are disconnected from your board's governing work can easily turn board members, superintendents, and senior administrators into unwitting victims of poor design, because they tend to:

- Lack what we call "horizontal discipline," chopping your board's governing work into narrow slices of district life that draw committee members' attention to parts of the district, rather than the whole, not unlike the proverbial blind man's defining an elephant as an ear, a trunk, a foot, or a leg. No single committee in this kind of board structure can attain the perspective of the whole district, and so full board meetings are the only place where the total picture can be seen, if at all.
- Turn board committees into operational or technical advisory committees rather than broad governing engines, virtually ensuring that critical governing judgments and decisions are not made

in a full and timely fashion, at the cost of your district underperforming and failing to fully meet students' needs.
- Build ownership of particular operational units and functions, thereby turning board members into advocates for particular operations and functions and breeding competition for resources at the board level, at the expense of the kind of broad governing decisions that take the district's and its students' overall best interests into account.
- Invite micromanagement and meddling in administrative detail and elicit a predictable defensive reaction from the superintendent and senior administrators.

Many of my readers have probably had the unfortunate and excruciating experience of sitting through, for example, a board personnel committee meeting at which deliberations focused on such non-governing questions as design of an employee evaluation form, the detailed employee recruitment process, the job description of the building maintenance director, and the process for orienting new employees. Devoid of any governing content, these questions invite

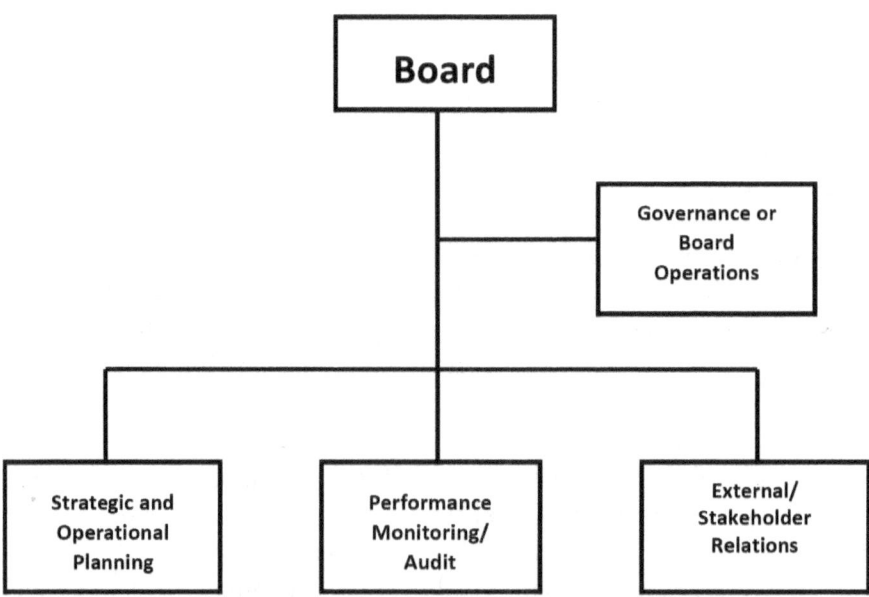

Figure 8.1. Standing Committee Organization

board members into the weeds, turning them into technical advisers and, worse, micromanagers, and they inevitably put superintendents on the defensive, as they attempt to defend pure managerial and administrative functions from board members' meddling. What a monumental waste of time!

A CLOSER LOOK AT WHAT WELL-DESIGNED COMMITTEES DO

The following capsule descriptions of the committees depicted in figure 8.1 will give you a sense of the work each regularly does.

The governance (or board operations) committee, headed by the board chair and consisting of the chairs of the other standing committees and the superintendent, is basically responsible for the effective functioning of the board, including board human resource development, and for the maintenance and development of the board-superintendent working relationship, in this capacity being accountable for functions such as:

- Coordinating the functioning of the board and its standing committees, keeping the board governing role updated, setting board member performance standards, and monitoring the performance of the board as a whole and of individual board members.
- Recommending revisions in the bylaws to the board in the interest of stronger governance and management.
- Developing and overseeing execution of a formal board member capacity-building program, including such elements as orientation of new members, continuing education and training, and a mentoring program pairing new with senior board members.
- Ensuring that the superintendent employment contract and position description are updated as necessary to reflect changing organizational needs, priorities, and circumstances.
- Annually negotiating superintendent performance targets, and annually or semiannually evaluating superintendent progress in achieving these targets.

The Strategic and Operational Planning Committee is accountable for designing and coordinating the board's participation in strategic and operational planning, including annual budget preparation, in this capacity:

- Reaching agreement with the superintendent on the detailed design of the planning and budget development cycle—with special attention to the board's role in planning—and on the annual planning calendar, and ensuring that the board participates fully and proactively in the planning process.
- Overseeing preparation for, and hosting, any board-superintendent-senior administrative team strategic work sessions that are held as part of the annual planning cycle.
- Recommending to the board the strategic issues that the district's detailed strategic planning should focus on, and reviewing and recommending to the board such critical planning products as updated values, vision, and mission statements, operational planning priorities, the annual budget, and other strategic and policy-level products that merit board attention.

The Performance Monitoring/Audit Committee is accountable for overseeing educational and financial performance, for updating operational policies and systems, and for overseeing the audit function, in this capacity:

- Reaching agreement with the superintendent on the key elements of an educational and financial reporting process, including the content, format, and frequency of performance reports to the board, and overseeing implementation of the process.
- Reviewing performance reports in committee meetings and reporting educational and financial performance to the board at its regular business meetings.
- Reviewing operational policies meriting the board's attention (such as policies to govern the accounting system and practices), identifying the need for revision, and recommending policy revisions to the full board.
- Presenting an overall assessment of the past year's educational and financial performance at annual strategic planning work sessions involving the full board.

- Processing procurement, contract, human resources, and other actions already in the annual budget.
- Sitting as the Audit Committee:

    1. Reviewing and approving the external audit firm selection process as recommended by the superintendent and selecting the external audit firm on the recommendation of the superintendent.
    2. Reviewing the external audit report, evaluating findings, and assessing recommendations submitted by the superintendent in response to the findings.
    3. Briefing the board on external audit findings and recommending action by the superintendent and the board in response to these findings.
    4. Monitoring the implementation of actions taken in response to the external audit report.
    5. Reviewing and evaluating on a continuing basis the financial management policies and procedures of the district and recommending updates as appropriate to the performance oversight and monitoring committee.

The external/stakeholder relations committee is responsible for maintaining effective communication and working relationships with the community in general and key district stakeholders such as local governments, for developing the annual legislative relations program and strategy, and for making sure that volunteer involvement in the district's affairs is highly productive and satisfying:

- Ensuring that the district's desired image is regularly updated.
- Overseeing the development and implementation of strategies for image building, marketing, and public relations and for maintaining close, positive relationships with key external stakeholders.
- Overseeing the development and implementation of legislative/governmental relations policies and strategies.
- Recommending to the board positions on legislative issues.
- Coordinating board members' speaking in appropriate forums on behalf of the district.

- Fashioning strategies and plans intended to enhance internal and external communication.
- Fashioning strategies and plans to promote nonboard volunteer involvement in providing input on the district's values, vision, strategic targets, and services.
- Monitoring volunteer involvement, identifying opportunities for improvement, and ensuring that such opportunities are taken into consideration in the planning process.

TESTED COMMITTEE OPERATING GUIDELINES

Experience has taught that formal guidelines governing committee operations will help to make them powerful "governing engines." These guidelines should be adopted by board resolution and periodically updated and fine-tuned. Three guidelines, in my experience, are especially critical in empowering standing committees.

1. Require That Every Board Member Serve on One and Only One Standing Committee

People are stretched so thin these days that it is just plain asking too much of volunteers to participate on more than one committee while also attending full board meetings; the inevitable result would be the kind of episodic and/or shallow participation that does not contribute to high-impact governing. Along with limiting board members to one standing committee, you should also make sure that every board member is assigned to a committee, with no exceptions. Otherwise, your board will be characterized by an unhealthy caste system that can damage board member morale and impede the development of a cohesive governing team: the "worker bee" board members who serve on committees, and the elite board members for whom committee participation is not required because their name alone is a sufficient contribution to governing.

2. Require That the Only Path to the Full Board Agenda Be through the Standing Committees and That All Reports and Recommendations Be Made by Standing Committee Chairs and Members

The surest way to ensure that your board's standing committees do not degenerate into discussion forums, spinning on and on without seriously influencing board deliberations, is to require that nothing gets on the board agenda without passing through the appropriate standing committee. This is like giving your committees a humongous calcium injection! And when you require that all reports and recommendations be made by committee chairs and members—not by staff—you not only ensure that committee members are well prepared for board meetings, but also provide them with ego satisfaction and build the credibility of the committees.

3. Regularly Rotate Committee Chairs and Members

By rotating board members among your standing committees, you ensure that every member on your board, at least if she sticks around for two terms, has an opportunity to become an expert in all of the major governing functions (planning, monitoring, external relations). Regular rotation also ensures that no board member becomes the official resident expert in—and owner of—a particular function, such as financial reporting or strategic planning, to whom everyone defers. Such unhealthy ownership impedes the development of other board members and, therefore, reduces the board's collective governing capacity. Experience has taught that a two-year committee term makes sense, providing enough time to learn the ropes in a particular functional area, while not allowing an unhealthy degree of ownership to develop.

ADAPTING THE MODEL STRUCTURE TO SMALLER BOARDS

Since many school boards are relatively small (often only five to seven members), a structure of three committees plus the governance (board operations) committee will obviously not work well. For a board of seven members, a solution that has worked well in practice is to fold the community/stakeholder relations committee into either the planning or performance-monitoring committee, resulting in a structure of two "bread and butter" standing committees plus the governance or board operations committee.

For a tiny board of only five members, actual standing committees would subdivide the board into units too small to have any credibility, so the practice of "virtual" committees has been successfully tested in recent years. A virtual committee is the board sitting as a committee of the whole, wearing the planning, performance monitoring, and community/stakeholder relations hats in separate sessions with a different board member serving as chair of each virtual committee. For example, two weeks before the regular board meeting, the committee of the whole meets for, let's say, three hours: one hour as the planning committee, one hour as the monitoring committee, and one hour as the community/stakeholder-relations committee. The virtual committees, while not as effective as a full-fledged standing committee, do keep the board focused on the broad governing streams and, hence, guard against the board's slipping into micromanagement.

9

HOW CAN WE TURN BOARD MEMBERS INTO SATISFIED OWNERS OF THEIR PLANNING WORK?

OWNER OR AUDIENCE?

I recently observed a school board-superintendent-senior administrative team work session that vividly demonstrated the power of ownership in action. This board's planning and development committee hosted the session, at which the committee chair presented the draft of an updated district values and vision statement and facilitated discussion. The superintendent and a couple of his top lieutenants participated, adding their observations at appropriate points, but it was clearly a committee-led event. The objective was to reach consensus on the draft, with any tweaks the majority of participating board members felt strongly about, and for the committee chair to move its acceptance at the next board business meeting in three weeks. The deliberations were a far cry from the traditional approach of thumbing through a finished document. The discussion was robust, and the questions participants raised were really pertinent. For example, there were lengthy, fascinating discussions about ways the school board could determine that values such as "district transparency" and "innovative educational solutions" were actually being observed in practice and how the board could reconcile "competing" values, such as the district's "commitment to efficiency and cost-consciousness" versus "investment in new, tested learning technologies."

The work session I was privileged to sit in on was the culmination of a four-month process kicked off by a daylong board-superintendent-senior administrative team "strategic planning retreat" that included active break-out-group engagement, including a group that brainstormed the elements that might make up an updated district values and vision statement. After the retreat, the planning and development committee fine-tuned the statement and then reviewed this second draft in two feedback sessions—one involving community leaders and the other a district task force involving faculty and administrators representing different buildings—that the committee used in coming up with the version they presented in the work session I observed. By the time the values and vision statement was unanimously adopted by resolution at the board meeting three weeks hence, I had no doubt this critical planning product—universally considered the driver of innovation-focused planning—was thoroughly owned by the board members, who testified that the process had been deeply satisfying: the polar opposite to the kind of passive-reactive process they'd grown accustomed to over the years.

Writing about this real-life case of transforming board members into satisfied owners of their governing work, I'm reminded of a contrasting case with a very different result. I heard various accounts of what happened while conducting one-on-one interviews with board members of another district, in preparation for a daylong "governance improvement work session." In a nutshell, a month or so before the interviews, the superintendent and her associate superintendent for institutional development teamed up to present a district strategic goals statement at the last board meeting that the senior administrators had put together in a "mini-retreat" a few weeks earlier. They'd crafted a thoughtful, polished document, which board members picked to pieces in the board meeting, behaving like the critical audience the process had turned them into. The resolution to adopt the goals statement and employ it to drive the upcoming strategic planning cycle was tabled. According to interviewees, the meeting ended on a sour note, with board members feeling frustrated at the all-too-familiar passive role they'd once again been forced to play. No one told me this, but I'm 99 percent sure the idea of the governance improvement work session was the direct result of this dispiriting experience.

CREATING SATISFIED BOARD OWNERS IS WELL WORTH THE EFFORT

This and the following chapter describe practical ways to transform school board members into truly satisfied owners of their governing work, drawing on recent experience in the rapidly evolving K–12 governance arena. This chapter focuses on the board's engagement in the district-planning function, and chapter 10 deals with the external/stakeholder relations function, including financial resource development. Board-savvy superintendents well know that they have a huge stake in fostering their board members' feelings of ownership and satisfaction, wearing a hat that is touched on in chapter 4: "chief governing process designer." Ownership and satisfaction breed commitment to particular governing products, such as a set of district innovation initiatives or the district's annual operating plan and budget. They also breed commitment to the superintendent, turning board members into reliable partners and allies who can be depended on to back the superintendent in tough times.

One of the most dramatic examples of ownership turning board members into reliable superintendent allies during a challenging time has to do with what is arguably the least-loved of all strategic initiatives in the K–12 sector: consolidating and closing schools. Parents and other residents of this suburban district were involved in a passionate love affair with their five neighborhood elementary schools; in fact, neighborhoods in this community were known by their schools' names. So when dramatic demographic change forced this district Strategic Governing Team to confront the challenge of moving from five to three elementary buildings, this board-savvy superintendent, donning the chief process designer hat, worked closely with the district board's planning committee in coming up with a detailed plan for moving forward on this perilous front, which was fleshed out over the course of three lengthy full board work sessions. Among other elements, the plan incorporated a series of neighborhood meetings to explain the demographic change driving the consolidation strategy that were jointly chaired by the board president and planning committee chair and included the superintendent, all five building principals, and the district CFO and associate superintendent for curriculum and instruction. This was clearly a board-driven strategy, and the fact that, despite a lot of vitriolic criticism of the superintendent, the board stayed firmly on course was without question due to board ownership of the process.

By the way, experience has taught that an important, but often ignored, spinoff benefit of transforming board members into satisfied owners is heightened community respect for the school board, and hence for the district itself. A board of lay leaders who play a strong, highly visible role in fashioning and carrying out initiatives such as building consolidation signal to community residents that their elected representatives on the board are actually in command, rather than being led around by the nose by controlling, manipulative administrators. In these days of widespread skepticism of public institutions and systems, demonstrably robust lay leadership has never been more important.

Board-savvy superintendents also know that board members' ownership of, and satisfaction in, their governing work doesn't just happen. It's essentially the result of meaningful board member engagement in shaping important governing decisions, and successful engagement depends on meticulous process design. So let's take a look at what's involved in mapping out the process for board members' engagement.

AN OVERVIEW OF PROCESS DESIGN

You'll recall that one of the benefits of well-designed board standing committees aligned with the board's broad governing functions that I touch on in chapter 8 is that standing committees can serve as a vehicle for mapping out board member engagement in their respective areas. For one thing, the informal setting of a committee meeting is much more conducive to board members, the superintendent, and senior administrators mapping out detailed processes, such as engaging board members in the annual operational planning and budget development process, than the more formal and public full board meeting could ever be. For another, the detailed knowledge and expertise that particular committees acquire in their respective functional sphere, such as external/stakeholder relations, are a valuable resource in designing engagement processes. So what do committee members, the superintendent, and senior administrators actually do when wearing their process designer hats?

The preeminent driver of committee process design is that board members' engagement should be meaningful, which involves three key elements:

1. Board member engagement should make a serious difference in terms of shaping important governing products. An example would be board engagement in the process of assessing potential district innovation initiatives and selecting the ones to be funded during the coming fiscal year. It's difficult to imagine any governing work more important in today's changing, challenging K–12 landscape.
2. Board member engagement should be technically sound, in terms of occurring at the right points in particular processes when there is a real opportunity to have serious impact on a governing product. Taking the innovation initiatives as an example, board members should be engaged early enough in the process to actually influence the choice of the initiatives that will be funded, rather than merely reviewing a staff-produced list of initiatives.
3. And the board member engagement process should be designed to capitalize on the resources board members bring to their governing work, such as experience, technical knowledge and expertise, and community ties.

THE CRITICAL ROLE OF THE SUPERINTENDENT AS CHIEF GOVERNING PROCESS DESIGNER

As each board standing committee's chief governing process designer, the superintendent plays four key roles:

1. Ensuring that the standing committees actually schedule sufficient time to carry out their process design function, in addition to their ongoing mainline responsibility of getting action recommendations and informational reports ready for the regular monthly board meeting. An approach that I've seen work very well is for a committee to set aside a half day toward the end of the fiscal year to working with the superintendent in updating

engagement processes for the upcoming year. For example, the performance-monitoring committee might work with the superintendent to upgrade the quarterly financial reporting process by adding bar charts on PowerPoint slides.
2. Providing committee members with pertinent information on developments in the functional area they are dealing with in process design. For example, in the area of innovation-focused planning, the superintendent will bring committee members up to speed on developments in this rapidly evolving area, such as the widespread abandonment of traditional comprehensive five-year planning, which has proved to be a total bust in terms of significant district innovation.
3. Bringing to the committee design process concrete recommendations that committee members can chew on, rather than relying on open-ended discussion that can so easily turn into ineffectual wheel-spinning. This doesn't mean that the superintendent should preempt committee members in playing their process design role, but she absolutely must provide enough technical input to ensure that the design process is productive.
4. Playing—or preparing the committee chair to play—a strong facilitator role in the design session, making sure the deliberations stay focused and produce the intended outcome: detailed processes for board engagement.

Now I'd like to examine some practical ways for transforming your board members into satisfied owners of their planning work via meaningful engagement.

THE GOLD STANDARD FOR BOARD PLANNING ENGAGEMENT

In recent years a very powerful change-focused planning logic and methodology have been developed and successfully tested that offer a tremendous opportunity for meaningful, high-impact board engagement. Popularly known as the "Change Investment Portfolio Process," it is run parallel to, and separate from, your district's business-as-usual operational planning/budget-development process, generating out-of-the-box change in the form of concrete projects that I call "change initiatives." These change initiatives are housed in your district's "Change Investment Portfolio," where they are pilot-tested and eventually mainstreamed into the annual budget and ongoing operations—or occasionally abandoned if they've proved unworkable.

Getting your school board actively involved in your district's portfolio process, especially at the open end of what I think of as the "change funnel," when you're brainstorming updated values and vision statements and identifying opportunities and challenges, will pay big dividends. After this point in the process, you'll want hands-on, intensive board involvement to give way to higher level board engagement, primarily overseeing progress, reviewing key planning products (such as the list of recommended issues to focus on during the current planning cycle), and monitoring the implementation of change initiatives. Experience has taught that there are three compelling reasons to make sure your board is intensively engaged early in the portfolio process.

First, your board members are uniquely qualified to provide critical substantive input early in the change-planning process, when your district is focusing on the big picture (e.g., vision, values, strategic issues). It's easy to take for granted—and if you're not careful, fail to fully capitalize on—the tremendous resources board members bring to the change game, such as diverse, in-depth leadership and executive experience, knowledge and expertise in all kinds of fields such as finance and law, status and credibility in the wider world, and connections with key stakeholders, including potential joint-venture partners. Second, no matter how change-savvy your superintendent is, and how enthusiastically and effectively she plays what you might call the "innovator-in-chief" role, she can't possibly get out-of-the box change accomplished without strong and steady board support throughout the portfolio process.

Second, formal board review and approval confers indispensable legitimacy to such critical planning outcomes as updated values and vision statements, the issues to be added to the Change Portfolio, and the change initiatives that have been fashioned to address the issues, laying a stronger foundation for accomplishing out-of-the-box change. And virtually 100 percent of boards possess the power of the purse, which means they must formally allocate the dollars required to carry out change initiatives. And finally, it's a rare innovator-in-chief who doesn't at one time or another in the process need board backing in dealing with staff resistance to change. It's important to keep in mind that commitment depends more on feelings of ownership than any other factor, and that the single best way to turn a key stakeholder such as your board into an owner is early involvement in shaping whatever it is you want owned. If your organization gets the board involved late in the portfolio process, when hands-on input isn't feasible, then you can't reasonably expect the board to feel firmly committed to the change initiatives in your district's portfolio.

Third, the portfolio process is so high-stakes in the context of our rapidly changing world—indeed, the preeminent key to your district's long-term stability and growth—and the work involved in updating your district's portfolio is so complex and challenging, that I think of the portfolio process as the "gold standard" for board engagement, as I observed earlier. I've found over the years that board members inevitably find dealing with such heady matters as updating values and vision and identifying issues fascinating, energizing, and tremendously satisfying. One of the important outcomes of such involvement at the open end of the change funnel is, therefore, a more solid board-superintendent working relationship, since productively engaged, satisfied board members inevitably make for better partners. Also keep in mind that the absence of early, meaningful board involvement in the portfolio process is a recipe for resentment and even alienation of board members, who cannot help but notice that they're being consigned to the periphery of an exciting, highly important planning initiative.

FOUR KEY STEPS IN THE PROCESS

Four key steps are involved in generating change initiatives that will be housed in your district's Change Portfolio:

1. Updating your district's Strategic Framework: its core values, vision for the long-range future, and strategic goals, and creating a fundamental foundation for the planning steps that follow, in terms of a set of overarching, predominantly ethical "rules of the game" to govern subsequent planning and operations, a desired

end state to lend purpose and direction to the planning, and operational and organizational boundaries that should be crossed only after very serious consideration. Involvement in updating your district's Strategic Framework is the preeminent means to turn your board members into ardent champions for, and satisfied owners of, out-of-the-box change.
2. Identifying out-of-the-box issues—"change challenges" (asking, *Should we take action to do something we're not currently doing?*)—in the form of opportunities to make progress in translating particular elements of your district's vision into reality and threats/challenges that will impede or threaten putting particular vision elements into practice.
3. Selecting the issues that your district intends to begin addressing *now*, by a process involving: (1) assessing the cost of *not* taking action to deal with a particular issue (direct, out-of-pocket costs such as a damaged reputation or a financial penalty, and foregone benefits, such as missing out on a major new grant opportunity); (2) estimating the likely cost of taking action (including time, money, and risk) and your district's capacity to take action; and (3) coming up with the issues that are likely to provide the most favorite cost/benefit ratio. These issues are added to your district's portfolio, where they are turned into change initiatives.
4. Fashioning change initiatives in the form of nuts-and-bolts projects to address the issues your district has selected, and adding these initiatives to your district's portfolio.

There is ample opportunity for meaningful board engagement in the first three steps of the portfolio process, under the leadership of your board's planning committee, but the fourth step mainly falls in the bailiwick of your administrators and faculty, under the superintendent's leadership.

A WORD ON ENGAGEMENT IN THE BUDGET PROCESS

One of the questions I always ask school board members in the one-on-one interviews I conduct in preparation for governance improvement projects is, "What you do you find least satisfying in your governing work?" To judge from the responses I've gotten over the years, board members' participation in the budget-preparation process tops the dissatisfaction list. One of the most common complaints goes like this: "We thumb through a finished tome asking a hodge-podge of questions focusing on relatively minor issues, and we really don't make much of a difference."

As a matter of fact, there isn't much of an opportunity to shape your district's annual operating plan and budget, certainly far less than in the Change Investment Portfolio process I describe above, for the simple reason that annual operational planning/budget development is a highly constrained process that basically involves incrementally tweaking and updating what is already going on in your district. Somewhere around 90 percent or more of your district's costs are fixed, so board members attempting to exert influence through manipulating dollars is a sure-fire recipe for frustration and an invitation to micromanage relatively minor objects of expenditure (district travel, supplies, grounds maintenance, and the like).

EXTRAORDINARY BUDGET OUTCOMES

Over the years I've observed board planning committees employ two approaches to engaging board members in shaping the district operating plan/budget. One way board members have been meaningfully engaged in the annual operational planning/budget-preparation process is, under the leadership of the board's planning committee, to identify the outcomes that that the budget document is intended to produce beyond the obvious one: tweaking and updating district programs and activities and the expenditure plan for the coming fiscal year. Then planning committee members can collaborate with the superintendent and senior administrators in designing the format of the budget document with an eye to achieving these outcomes. The outcomes discussion that took place in one board budget outcomes work session hosted by the board's planning committee that I observed a year or so ago was a real eye-opener for participating board members. They hadn't previously given much thought to outcomes that the budgeting process and the budget document itself were intended to produce, beyond the obvious need to have a detailed annual plan for district expenditures in place that were in balance with projected district revenues.

For example, everyone agreed pretty quickly that the adopted budget—at least in summary form—could be a powerful tool for educating the public at large and key stakeholders like the chamber of commerce and city and county governments on district priorities, goals, and finances. And they could see that, if properly presented, the budget document might also promote the district's image as a prudent steward of precious financial resources and as an efficient, well-managed public institution. It wasn't a big jump from local stakeholders to regional and national foundations, which might be more receptive to district funding proposals on the basis of a well-crafted budget document that painted a picture of an innovative, accountable, soundly managed educational enterprise. So very close attention was paid to the messages conveyed in the introduction to the budget, and to the appearance of the budget document, in order to achieve these very special outcomes.

THE PREBUDGET OPERATIONAL PLANNING WORK SESSION

Another very effective way school board planning committees have spearheaded effective board member engagement in shaping the annual operating plan/budget is to design and host a special board "prebudget" work session aimed at educating board members about major districtwide administrative units (e.g., the curriculum and instruction and pupil services departments) and at surfacing and examining particular educational and managerial issues of special interest to board members. Without question, the details in the typical budget document can overwhelm your board members, seriously handicapping them in contributing to the operational planning process, and so the challenge is to help board members rise above this mountain of detail, homing in on critical factors and issues that board members should be aware of. In my experience, the prebudget work session can do a very effective job of raising board members' sights and making them far more insightful reviewers of the finished operating plan/budget.

The prebudget work sessions I've sat in on typically last the better part of a day and involve the superintendent and the associate superintendents and districtwide administrative unit heads making presentations, using PowerPoint slides, and answering board members' questions. The following presentation outline is representative of a number of work sessions I've participated in over the years—covering each administrative unit's:

- Mission
- Organizational structure
- Current budget by major cost categories
- Current performance objectives/targets
- Track record in achieving these objectives/targets thus far this year, highlighting significant performance shortfalls and exemplary performance
- Major operational issues
- Proposed major performance objectives/targets for the coming fiscal year
- High-priority managerial and programmatic changes being considered for the coming fiscal year
- Significant expenditure increases—or significant new expenditures—being contemplated, linked with specific performance objectives/targets and management changes

One prebudget work session I sat in on a few years ago not only generated robust, often-illuminating discussion and energized participating board members, but also produced a short list of operational issues that were eventually highlighted in the finished operating plan/budget submitted to the planning committee for review and eventually to the full board. For example, one of the issues explored in depth at this district board's prebudget work session was security, not only of buildings but also at district events such as athletic contests. So the plan and budget for security was highlighted in the budget submission. By the way, a side benefit of this and other similar work sessions I've observed is a more cohesive Strategic Governing Team as a result of spending a whole day together intensively exploring critical issues.

10

HOW CAN WE TURN BOARD MEMBERS INTO SATISFIED OWNERS OF THEIR EXTERNAL/STAKEHOLDER RELATIONS WORK?

A DAUNTING CHALLENGE

If the parents of our students were our districts' only "paying customers," public school districts wouldn't face such a daunting public relations and image building challenge. But local taxpayers, the majority of whom these days don't have children in public school classrooms, pay a large part of the local share of the K–12 tab, and these paying customers can be a really hard sell. For one thing, many of them appear to share the widespread distrust of public institutions, and unless they happen to have kids in the public schools, they're unlikely to know much about what's going on in their public school district educationally or administratively.

"Guaranteeing teachers job security is why they aren't more creative in the classroom, and one of the big reasons why we've got to have more charter schools." "Increasing educational funding would be throwing good money after bad." I doubt if my readers would agree with these two comments, but I hear variations of them frequently. What always worries me is not just what's being said, but who's doing the talking. I'm recounting what I've heard over the years from people who, while you and I might think them wrong-headed, I've often found bright, well-educated, and generally thoughtful. They're living proof of three maxims at the heart of this chapter. The first is that the good work your district does never has and never will speak for itself. If in reality action always did speak louder than words, school districts wouldn't have to devote so much attention to spreading the word on their valuable contribution to the quality of life and economic well-being of their communities.

The second maxim at the heart of this chapter is that if your district doesn't take the initiative in building a positive community image, critics will be more than happy to take on the job. And if you allow them to, they've got the social media tools these days to easily raise questions about the quality of your educational endeavors and the effectiveness of your management practices. And the third maxim is that impressions are facts. This is to say that what people believe to be true is true, in their eyes anyway. Taken together these maxims make a powerful case for public school districts to treat external relations and image building as a top-tier function. And if the negative comments I've frequently heard over the years are any indication, public education must grapple with a serious image problem.

THERE'S SOME GOOD NEWS—BUT . . .

The good news, I'm pleased to report, is that an increasing number of school districts around the country appear to be paying serious attention to external relations generally, and specifically to image building and stakeholder relationship management. By "serious" attention, I mean taking such steps as recruiting a top professional to serve as the district's public relations or public information officer, producing a handsome annual report, taking advantage of social media to reach community members, booking the superintendent and senior administrators to speak in community forums, and the like. These are significant steps on the public relations front, but all too often they leave a critical ingredient out of the recipe for effective district image building: active board member engagement.

I'm not sure why so few school board members have been actively engaged in the obviously critical external/stakeholder relations arena, but two factors are likely to account for the lack of board member engagement. For one thing many board members arrive at the boardroom seeing themselves as representatives of the constituencies that put them there, not of the school district they've been elected to govern, and they all too often bring with them the infamous "watch-the-critters-so-they-don't-steal-the-store" mentality, which turns them into internal critics rather than district advocates. For another, in my experience many if not most superintendents and their senior administrators don't really welcome active school board involvement in external affairs, doubting that they are sufficiently willing and able to acquit themselves well in in the external relations arena. Whatever the reasons, school districts all over the country are failing to capitalize on their board members as a precious resource on the external relations and image building front, at a steep cost in terms of reduced public support.

A COMPELLING CASE FOR BOARD ENGAGEMENT

Your school board members are in a unique position to make a significant contribution—through both their governing work and their non-governing, hands-on diplomatic and image-building activities—to strengthening your district's public image and building its relationships with critical constituents and stakeholders. Their position on the school board gives them unique visibility and clout. Not only are they perceived as important community leaders, but they are also seen as above the fray and less captive to the system they are responsible for governing than the superintendent and her administrative team. School board members also bring with them to the boardroom strong community contacts and affiliation networks and familiarity with the people who elected them. They are woven into the fabric of the community, rather than observing it from a distance, and this uniquely equips your board members to reach out, capturing minds and hearts on behalf of the public schools.

There's another important reason to get your school board members meaningfully engaged in the external relations and image-building function: the work tends to be interesting, enjoyable, and frequently ego satisfying—and hence a form of nonmonetary compensation for all the time they spend in the boardroom grappling with difficult and often negative issues. Experience has taught me that satisfied board members make for not only more productive members of a district's Strategic Governing Team, but also more reliable partners for the superintendent. I vividly recall chatting with a board member after she'd spoken about her district's strategic goals and educational programs at a chamber of commerce luncheon meeting. I was aware that when she was initially approached by the superintendent to speak at the upcoming luncheon, she was very reluctant, doubting—as she shared with the superintendent—that she was experienced enough at the podium to do an adequate job of representing the district and her board colleagues. Of course, she was almost certainly also afraid she might be embarrassed in playing an unfamiliar role, and we all know that embarrassment sounds worse than death to many people.

To make what could be a long story short, the superintendent and his public information officer pitched in to prepare her for the speaking engagement, supplying her with talking points and a few PowerPoint slides, and even an opportunity to do a dry run in the superintendent's conference room with several administrators and board members making up her audience. Well, the assistance payed off handsomely. She took the podium knowing her stuff inside-out, made a very interesting presentation, and comfortably answered several questions. She also tossed a few questions to the district public information officer, who was sitting at her side. When I chatted with her afterward, she was glowing. And, by the way, the glow didn't wear off anytime soon, and it was obvious from her behavior in the ensuing months that she'd become a closer, more supportive colleague of the superintendent's. Never doubt that nonmonetary compensation can make a real difference.

GOVERNING VERSUS DOING

This chapter describes two paths board members travel on the external relations/image-building road: governing the external/image-building function, and participating in actually doing external relations and image-building work. A caveat is in order here. School board members, being for the most part unpaid, part-time volunteers with busy lives beyond the board, can bring only so much time and energy to their primary responsibility: doing high-impact governing work that makes a significant positive difference in your district's affairs. Your district cannot afford for board members to become so immersed in doing nongoverning work that their governing role is diluted. This will always be a clear and present danger for the simple reason that nongoverning work, such as speaking at a luncheon meeting or meeting with a key stakeholder representative, tends to be enjoyable and ego satisfying and often far less stressful than grappling with thorny strategic and policy-level issues.

Maintaining the proper balance between governing and nongoverning work would typically fall in the bailiwick of the kind of board governance or board operations committee that is described in chapter 8. This committee is often assisted by a standing external/stakeholder relations committee with explicit responsibility for overseeing this governing function. Maintaining the right balance is a much easier task, in my experience, when the new board member orientation program makes a very clear distinction between the primary governing work of the board and the nongoverning activities board members will be engaged in. Blurring the line separating these two kinds of board work makes maintaining the proper balance extremely difficult.

LAYING THE FOUNDATION FOR MEANINGFUL BOARD MEMBER ENGAGEMENT

Before we get into the specific roles that your district's board members can productively play in the external relations and image building area, you should be aware of three essential foundation stones for meaningful engagement: a standing committee to serve as a structural home for the function, formal school board commitment to the external relations/image-building role, and strong support from the superintendent and senior administrators. Without a board standing committee planning for and overseeing the external affairs function, it is highly unlikely to be treated in practice as a serious board priority. For one thing, there wouldn't be a practical mechanism for fashioning engagement strategy or a forum to discuss implementation and tweak strategies. In chapter 8 you'll find a detailed description of such a committee, which is often called "external/stakeholder relations." Without a structural home bringing together board members, the superintendent, and key administrators around the same table, inevitable day-to-day operational pressures and crises would probably sink the external relations ship fairly early in its maiden voyage.

School board members must be firmly committed to playing an affirmative role in reaching out to the wider community if their engagement in the external arena is to succeed, and this commitment should be formalized by resolution and incorporated into the board's policy manual. One way to handle this is for the board's governance or board operations committee (see chapter 8) to make sure that the board's "governing mission" includes an explicit statement about the role, such as: "Board members will play an active role in promoting our district's image in the community and building positive working relationships with key community stakeholders." Participation in the external relations function can also be built into the board member performance targets established by the governance or board operations committee. For example, one school board added to its performance targets: "Board members are expected to speak on behalf of our district in selected community forums at least four times a year."

And for board members to succeed in the external relations and image-building arena, the superintendent and senior administrators must really want them to play the role and be committed to providing them with the support required for them to succeed. A key piece of the support puzzle is a district public relations (often called "public information") officer explicitly responsible for working with the board's external/stakeholder relations committee and for making sure board members are adequately supported. Support will include collecting information on important speaking opportunities, developing PowerPoint presentations and other material that board members can use in speaking engagements, and even orchestrating speaker rehearsal sessions.

GOVERNING IN THE AREA OF IMAGE BUILDING

Your board's external/stakeholder relations committee will take the lead in developing three important governing products in its sphere of responsibility, in close collaboration with the superintendent and her top administrators: a district image statement, an image-building strategy, and a stakeholder relationship-building strategy. Your district's image statement provides you with the key messages you want to get out to your community and in fashioning image-building strategies. Without knowing—in real detail—how you want your school system to be perceived in the community generally and by particular constituencies and stakeholder groups specifically, you couldn't possibly do a good job of determining the messages your district needs to convey publicly. Although your district image statement plays a key role in fashioning external relations strategies, it is basically an internal tool. Unlike your district's vision statement or mission, it would never be published or explicitly quoted in presentations in community forums. Its presence would be felt indirectly, through your district's image building efforts.

A very effective approach to fashioning a detailed district image statement is to brainstorm the image elements in a board-superintendent-senior administrator retreat, at which a breakout group might fashion the statement by completing the sentence, "We need/want our district to be seen as. . . ." Subsequently, the image statement might be tweaked and polished by the superintendent and senior administrators and massaged to the board's external/stakeholder relations committee. Real-life image statements district Strategic Governing Teams have developed have included such elements as "doing a top-quality job of educating our students," "welcoming the active involvement of our students' parents," "being open and responsive to the community," "making a major contribution to the quality of life in our community," "prudently managing financial and other resources," "fostering creative partnerships with community institutions," and the like.

With the image statement in hand, the superintendent and his senior administrators can go about the business of developing concrete, detailed image-building strategies to review with the board external/stakeholder relations committee, such as adopting an updated district logo, revamping the annual report to the community, upgrading the district website, and getting out the key messages in the image statement by such means as booking board members to speak in community forums. When reviewing the strategies proposed by the superintendent and senior administrators, the board's external/stakeholder relations committee should take responsibility for determining whether key elements of the district image are being adequately addressed. For example, examining the key messages being conveyed on the upgraded website, committee members might ask such questions as, "Are we effectively getting across the message that our district is making a huge contribution to our community's quality of life and its economic development?" "Is the importance we place on prudently managing the tax dollars we receive being clearly conveyed?"

GOVERNING IN THE AREA OF STAKEHOLDER RELATIONS

In the area of stakeholder relations, your board's external/stakeholder relations committee's primary governing role is to work with the superintendent and senior administrators in fashioning a detailed stakeholder relations strategy and to oversee its execution. Before getting into the details, this is the appropriate place to remind you who stakeholders are. Generally speaking, a district stakeholder is any person, group of people or formal organization that it makes sense to build and manage a relationship with because something important is at stake in the relationship—money, political support, technical assistance, legitimacy, and the like. Our subject in this chapter is external stakeholders outside of your district's structure, and my focus is specifically formal organizations, such as local governments, nonprofit corporations, civic associations, postsecondary institutions, and print and broadcast media, to name some of the more important. Effective management of key stakeholder relationships is so critical to the health of public school districts that it's now universally accepted that stakeholder relations is a top-tier board governing priority and a preeminent superintendent leadership target.

The normal starting point for fashioning or updating your district's stakeholder relations strategy is to conduct a preliminary stakeholder analysis, which is often accomplished in a board-superintendent-senior administrator retreat, going through the following steps:

- Make a list of stakeholders in the community with which it makes sense for your district to maintain some kind of relationship.
- Identify the stakes involved for your district in each of the relationships, and select the ten to fifteen stakeholders involving the highest stakes.
- For these ten to fifteen top-tier stakeholders, analyze each relationship, asking: What does our district want from the relation-

ship? What do we think the stakeholder expects in return to keep the relationship healthy?
- Finally, assess each relationship in terms of how close, positive, and productive it is, and identify any relationship problems that stand out.

Following up on the retreat work, the superintendent and her administrative team might fashion for review with your board's external/stakeholder relations committee a detailed stakeholder relationship-management strategy, which might consist of: the district's major objectives for each relationship (e.g., turning the mayor into a strong supporter of the district's upcoming capital improvement bond issue), and the action plan for achieving each objective (e.g., hold a luncheon meetings involving the mayor, school board president, and superintendent to discuss the bond issue; invite the mayor to chair the bond issue steering committee). Of course, your board's external/stakeholder relations committee will oversee implementation of the strategy, tweaking it as necessary based on experience.

YOUR BOARD'S NONGOVERNING, HANDS-ON WORK

In my experience, the three most productive strategies for hands-on, nongoverning board involvement in the external arena are: a board speakers bureau, board member facilitation of community forums, and board member participation in maintaining particularly high-priority stakeholder relationships. The board speakers bureau is a simple, high-yield approach that can serve your district as a powerful communication vehicle while also providing board members with an enjoyable, ego-satisfying experience. Community groups typically appreciate senior administrators making the effort to address them, but presentations by unpaid board members tend to have much higher-impact in terms of relationship building. In my experience, the following two elements will ensure that your district's board speakers bureau functions effectively as an image-building tool:

- Oversight and coordination by your board's external/stakeholder relations committee, including identifying high-priority commu-

nity forums, enlisting board members to speak and matching them with appropriate forums, and providing board speakers with the key messages to be conveyed in specific forums.
- Strong executive support from the superintendent and senior administrators, such as developing specific presentation points, putting together a PowerPoint presentation, providing appropriate handout material, and staging a "dress rehearsal" for board speakers who are interested.

Having board members chair or facilitate a community forum on behalf of your district can be a powerful image builder, demonstrating publicly that board members really do care about community relations and communicating your district's openness and responsiveness by inviting the community to participate in important school business. For example, districts have invited community members to participate in fleshing out district values and vision statements and other planning products that were originally brainstormed in a district board retreat. Typically, members of the board's planning committee have facilitated these sessions.

Building and maintaining relationships with key stakeholders is an immense challenge in light of the number of stakeholder relationships to manage, so there is always a need for board member participation to take some of the pressure off the superintendent and top administrators. For example, one of your board members might serve as a formal liaison with the chamber of commerce, in this capacity: actively participating in chamber affairs (perhaps even becoming a member of the chamber board, representing your district); making sure that district priorities, activities, and positions on specific issues are well understood by the chamber; and alerting the school board's external/stakeholder relations committee of relationship problems that need to be addressed.

A CLOSING LOOK AT THE DISTRICT-EDUCATIONAL FOUNDATION RELATIONSHIP

Many public school districts around the country have played a part in establishing an educational foundation to raise money, frequently to support educational innovation initiatives. An educational foundation is by definition an independent nonprofit (501[c][3]) corporation with its own governing board that is not part of the school district's structure, although its board might include school district representation. Of course, an educational foundation will succeed at fund raising only to the extent that it builds a truly high-level board that can access financial resources. Since heavy-hitter board members rightly expect to have impact as foundation governors, it's not uncommon to find a school board and foundation board in conflict, typically over how the foundation board makes grants to the district.

I witnessed the conflict first-hand a few years ago when I'd been retained to facilitate a discussion about my client school district's relationship with the local educational foundation. The tension in the conference room was palpable as the meeting began. The superintendent and her board president at one end of the table were glaring at the educational foundation CEO and his board chair at the other end. I sat in the middle between the two "camps." The school board president kicked off the discussion on a positive note, expressing the district's appreciation for the foundation's efforts to raise money for district educational initiatives and to build wider community support for the district. Then he homed in on the issue that'd led to this pretty dramatic negotiating session: that the foundation CEO and his staff had started making innovation grants directly to faculty applicants, without going through any kind of district vetting.

I recall the school board president saying something along these lines: "We really need financial support, and we think it's great you're bringing new resources into the district, but it'd be really chaotic for your staff to deal directly with our faculty and put money into projects that don't fit into our educational priorities and plans." The foundation board chair, clearly offended, responded by pointing out that the foundation had built a board of real heavy-hitters—business and nonprofit CEOs with access to substantial financial resources—who were passionately committed to public education. "Not only should you appreciate what we're doing for the schools, but you should also respect the board we've put together," was what I recall him saying.

I'm happy to report that this story has a happy ending: the superintendent and foundation CEO worked out a simple and somewhat obvious solution that had proposals for funding go through the superintendent's office to the foundation, after having been vetted internally. And the superintendent wisely sweetened the deal by inviting the foundation board chair and CEO to attend the district's annual board–administrative team strategic planning retreat, at which educational priorities were updated and high-stakes issues identified and analyzed. But what struck me is that the dramatic confrontation in the boardroom could easily have been avoided if the district had taken the initiative—spearheaded by the board's community relations committee—in building a mutually satisfying and productive working relationship with the foundation early in the foundation's life, when the situation was still fluid.

What I've seen work very well is for the district's board president and superintendent to produce a formal relationship document, spelling out the district's expectations and ground rules vis-à-vis the new foundation before lines have hardened. Such a document, which, of course, could easily be turned into a formal district-foundation agreement, should map out how proposals for foundation funding will be developed within the district structure and submitted to the foundation.

11

HOW CAN WE ENGAGE SENIOR ADMINISTRATORS IN THE GOVERNING PROCESS?

FULLY REALIZING THE TREMENDOUS GOVERNING POTENTIAL OF BOARD COMMITTEES

Experience has taught me that board standing committees are the name of the game in terms of meaningful engagement of your district's senior administrators in the governing function. Therefore, this concluding chapter focuses on practical steps your district's Strategic Governing Team can take to ensure that you capitalize on well-designed board standing committees as highly effective governing engines. As chapter 8 makes clear, board standing committees that are aligned with the board's broad streams of governing decisions and judgments are the drivers of the kind of high-impact governing that makes a tremendous difference in the affairs of your district. This is the case whether your board employs full-fledged standalone committees that hold separate meetings or whether they are what I call "virtual" committees: the full board holding a committee-of-the-whole work session divided into committee segments. You'll recall that in chapter 8 I recommend that each committee-of-the-whole segment of the work session be chaired by a different board member. The virtual committee approach is a thoroughly tested way that a small board of five or fewer members can reap most of the governing benefits of well-designed committees without creating such small standalone committees that they lack legitimacy.

As chapters 8 and 9 demonstrate, successfully implementing a structure of well-designed board standing committees will pay off handsomely for your district. The most obvious benefits include:

- More productive board meetings as a result of standing committee preparation.
- Board members' acquisition of governing knowledge and skills from participating in committee deliberations, especially when board members are rotated regularly among the standing committees.
- Enhanced board member satisfaction in, and commitment to, their governing work.
- Preservation of the superintendent's line of credit with the board as a result of committee chairs' presenting all action recommendations and informational reports at regular board business meetings.

You'll recall that chapter 9 pays close attention to an often-neglected but truly powerful role of standing committees: transforming board members into strong owners of their governing work by designing processes that meaningfully engage board members in such governing functions as strategic and operational planning and budget development. And you'll also recall that the superintendent, wearing her "chief governing process designer" hat, plays the leading role in mapping out these processes with committee members, ensuring that their process design work capitalizes on the most recent advances in the art of governance.

BEATING THE ODDS

This concluding chapter offers detailed, practical guidance that has been thoroughly tested in practice for successfully launching and institutionalizing a structure of well-designed standing committees. I focus on getting committees firmly established—up and running smoothly—and on providing the ongoing administrative support your committees will require to continue performing at a high-level over the long run. As

HOW CAN WE ENGAGE SENIOR ADMINISTRATORS IN THE GOVERNING PROCESS?

my readers well know, designing a new structure to replace outmoded "silo" committees is one thing; putting the new committees into actual practice and keeping them running productively over the long run is entirely another.

Getting a new committee structure up and running can be a daunting challenge primarily because normal human beings tend to resist significant change. In fact, I've learned over the course of my thirty years of work in the public/nonprofit sector that significant, planned change often bites the dust because people prefer the security and comfort of the familiar (e.g., the old-time silo committees or no committees at all) to venturing onto new terrain (the new committees) that feels extremely uncomfortable and dangerous, in the sense that they might fail to meet the demands of the new committees.

And even when a new committee structure is fully functional, board members—part-time volunteers who have limited time and turn over continuously—can't be expected to carry the ball and keeping it running well. The responsibility—and burden—falls squarely on the superintendent and her senior administrators. Three primary keys that I'll be discussing in detail in this concluding chapter will ensure that you get your new board committees off to a good start and keep them humming along as powerful governing engines:

1. A really board-savvy superintendent at the helm who is immersed in all of the details involved in launching and supporting the new standing committees.
2. A temporary program dedicated to getting the new committees firmly launched.
3. A permanent structure for managing ongoing administrative support to the new committees once they are launched.

A BOARD-SAVVY SUPERINTENDENT AT THE HELM

The truly board-savvy superintendents I've worked with over the years in putting a new committee structure in place have understood how critical well-designed standing committees are to their board's governing performance, and they have been keenly aware that their partnership with the board heavily depends on these well-designed committees, primarily because of their partnership with committee chairs. Understanding that transforming new committees into firmly established, smoothly operating governing engines is likely to be technically and politically challenging, they play a highly visible, active role in making sure the committees get off to a good start and succeed over the long run. They do not delegate institutionalizing the new committees to one of their lieutenants and look on from a distance.

The reality is that resistance can be so intense that only the superintendent has the clout to overcome it, especially in the committees' infancy. I saw this first-hand recently, when a couple of old-guard board members spoke up in the orientation session for new committee chairs and members, strongly urging that the board rescind the decision to place the budget-preparation function in the new planning and development committee and place it in the new performance-monitoring committee, speciously arguing the financial monitoring and budgeting functions needed to be closely attached. I am convinced that this wrong-headed backward step might have been taken if the superintendent hadn't strongly defended the integrity of the new structure. And I should add that the few times I have seen a new committee structure come unraveled, the primary cause has been superintendent inattention.

LAUNCHING A NEW COMMITTEE STRUCTURE

Getting a new standing committee structure well-launched involves six key steps: (1) formally establishing the new committees' legitimacy; (2) creating a temporary program to oversee and manage implementation of the new committees; (3) putting together a committee implementation plan; (4) choosing the right chairs to head the new committees; (5) assigning senior administrative team members to serve as "chief staff liaisons" to the new committees; and (6) conducting a thorough orientation for board and administrative team members on the new committees.

ESTABLISHING NEW COMMITTEE LEGITIMACY

Establishing the new committees' legitimacy can be simply accomplished by your school board adopting one or more resolutions. A school board I worked with recently, for example, adopted a resolution resolving that four new standing committees be adopted as the "governing structure" of the board and that implementation of the new committees "adhere" to detailed committee functional descriptions appended to the resolution. Some school boards and other public/nonprofit organizations have specified standing committees in their bylaws. I do not recommend this since it makes sense for boards to be able to tweak and update their standing committee structure without having to go through the process of amending the bylaws.

TEMPORARY COMMITTEE IMPLEMENTATION PROGRAM AND PLAN

Several school boards have established a temporary program (one district called it the "High-Impact Governing Program") with a steering committee to oversee and manage implementation of the new committees. Often headed by the board chair and consisting of the other board officers and the superintendent, this steering committee typically adopts a committee implementation plan prepared by the superintendent or a governance consultant, and oversees carrying the plan out. Milestones in typical implementation plans include appointing new committee chairs and members, designating the chief staff liaisons to the new committees, conducting an orientation on the new structure for all board and administrative team members, and putting in place a formal administrative support structure and process to ensure effective committee functioning. The program steering committee is typically phased out when the board's new governance or board operations committee becomes fully functional and is capable of overseeing and coordinating standing committee operations.

THE RIGHT NEW COMMITTEE CHAIRS

Whether newly created committees find their sea legs early in their existence and are soon firmly established depends heavily on the temporary program steering committee recommending to the board chair the appointment of the right board members to chair the new committees. Once the new committees have effectively functioned for a year, the appointment of committee chairs is a more routine matter. Experience has taught that the most effective chairs of new standing committees:

- Bring stature to the job: having been high-performing, influential board members who command the respect of their peers.
- Relate to, and are passionately committed to, the committee's role and responsibilities.
- Bring pertinent knowledge and experience to the committee.
- Are able and willing to commit the time to chairing the committee.
- Bring strong facilitative skills to the job.

A serious mismatch between a chair and her new committee can exact a high cost in terms of the committee getting off on the wrong foot and losing credibility among its members. I vividly recall such a case, when the chair of the newly created planning and development committee brought minimal interest in planning process to his new chairmanship. Since the planning function involves a tremendous amount of process design and management, this lack of interest seriously set back the committee's development and damaged its credibility.

COMMITTEE CHIEF STAFF LIAISONS

Just as important as the board chair's appointment of the right new standing committee chairs is the superintendent's appointment of an executive team member to serve as "chief staff liaison" to each of the committees. Responsible to the superintendent, board chair (as chair of the governance or board operations committee), and the committee chair, the chief staff liaison is essentially accountable for ensuring that her committee is well-staffed and that her committee chair is strongly supported and is successful in leading committee deliberations. The chief staff liaison's responsibilities include:

- Developing future committee agendas.
- Reviewing future committee agendas with the senior administrative team sitting as the Governance Coordinating Committee and his or her standing committee chair.

- Ensuring that his or her committee chair is well-prepared to lead committee deliberations.
- Preparing for a regularly scheduled session of the senior administrative team sitting as the "Governance Coordinating Committee" dedicated to supporting the board and its standing committees (the chief staff liaison is responsible for leading discussion of upcoming committee agendas at these meetings and for facilitating agreement on administrative team responsibilities for preparing material for upcoming standing committee meetings).
- Overseeing the preparation of written material and oral briefings for committee meetings, in this capacity exercising rigorous quality control and making sure that written materials are transmitted well in advance of committee meetings (note: this does *not* mean preparing all of the material, but it does mean making sure that material of high quality is transmitted to the committee).
- Following up on standing committee meetings by preparing the standing committee report to the full board, including for information and for action items (note: this responsibility cannot be delegated to administrative support staff).

ORIENTATION ON THE NEW COMMITTEES

A thorough understanding of the rationale for—and the roles and functions of—the committees making up the new structure has proved to be critical to their getting off on the right foot, so a well-designed orientation program is an important implementation milestone. The most effective orientation programs I have seen involve all board and administrative team members in a three- to four-hour session at which, using PowerPoint slides:

- The board chair provides participants with background and context: reviewing the steps involved in creating the new committees (e.g., a governance retreat followed by an action report and adoption of enabling resolutions in a special work session), presenting the rationale for the new structure (e.g., to align committees with broad governing functions in order to strengthen board governing performance), and describing key principles undergirding the

structure (e.g., active board member engagement, a solid board-superintendent partnership, committees' presentation of all recommendations and reports at board meetings, rotation of committee chairs and members, etc.).
- Each committee chair teams up with her committee's chief staff liaison to present the committee's role and detailed functions.
- The superintendent describes the functions of the chief staff liaisons.
- The board chair and superintendent spend an hour addressing any questions participants have.

THE ONGOING ADMINISTRATIVE GOVERNANCE SUPPORT STRUCTURE AND PROCESS

Many districts have established the Administrative Governance Support Structure that is described below, for the express purpose of managing the process of developing agendas and materials for meetings of the new standing committees and managing follow-up to committee meetings, ensuring that:

- Committees are engaged in interesting and productive work for which committee members feel strong ownership.
- Committee chairs truly own agenda items and are well-prepared to lead meetings.
- Quality control is rigorously maintained in the development of agendas and other documentation for standing committee meetings.
- The reports to the board following up on standing committee meetings—which are prepared by the chief staff liaisons to the standing committees—clearly describe informational and action items and provide an accurate summary of major points made in committee meetings (these reports are not traditional "he said/she said" minutes—see below).

A formal structure might seem a bit bureaucratic at first blush, but experience has taught that it is the best way to counter the inevitable centrifugal force generated by Type-A committee chairs who expect to produce results. The Administrative Governance Support Structure ensures that the superintendent and senior administrative team stay well ahead of the game and are not thrown on the defensive. The last thing the superintendent and her senior administrators need is for standing committee chairs to charge ahead in fashioning their own agendas to address their own pet issues, outstripping staff and throwing them on the defensive.

The Administrative Governance Support Structure typically consists of the following three elements:

1. A central role for the committee chief staff liaisons.
2. Regular meetings of the senior administrative team sitting as the "Governance Coordinating Committee" that are dedicated to governance matters, principally reviewing agenda items for upcoming standing committee meetings (the superintendent always chairs these meetings, and the chief staff liaisons lead discussion of upcoming standing committee agendas).
3. An ongoing standing committee agenda development and follow-through process.

The agenda development and follow-through process typically consists of the following steps:

- Chief staff liaisons prepare drafts of the agendas for upcoming standing committee meetings, based on touching base with the appropriate senior administrators relative to the informational and action items needing standing committee attention.
- The chief staff liaisons review these draft agendas with the senior administrative team sitting as the Governance Coordinating Committee.
- The chief staff liaisons then review the revised agendas with their standing committee chairs, securing their buy-in and making sure they understand each item on the agenda.
- The chief staff liaisons prepare drafts of their respective standing committees' follow-through reports to the board, review the reports with the superintendent, revising the reports as appropriate, and then review the reports with the committee chairs, making further revisions as appropriate.

- The governance or board operations committee meets to finalize the board agenda, reaching agreement on the approximate allocation of time to each standing committee, depending on each committee's action and information items being sent to the board. The chief staff liaisons should always participate in these meetings.
- As appropriate, the chief staff liaisons meet with their respective standing committee chairs again before the board meeting to go over the content of committee reports, making sure the chairs are well-prepared to present items at the board meeting.

One of the typical responsibilities of the chief staff liaisons is to draft the official report to the board from their respective committees for the upcoming board meeting. In my experience, effective standing committee reports:

- Are divided into two main sections: "For Information" and "For Action."
- Clearly describe each action that will be recommended at the upcoming board meeting and provide highlights of the discussion leading to the decision to recommend each action.
- Provide briefer summary information on informational items.

These standing committee reports are typically not traditional detailed minutes of the "she said/he said" variety. If a district determines that formal, traditional minutes are required for standing committee meetings (in my experience, minutes are typically not required), the chief staff liaisons can still prepare the standing committee reports to the board with the minutes appended for anyone wanting to look them over. Of course, the chief staff liaisons will want to review their standing committee reports with the superintendent and committee chairs before they are finalized and transmitted to the board as part of the monthly business meeting packet.

CONCLUDING THOUGHTS: MEETING THE GOVERNING CHALLENGE

Writing this book has been a passionate endeavor for me for a number of reasons. Personally, I am indebted to public education—the Vandalia

(Illinois) Community School District and later the University of Illinois at Urbana-Champaign—for laying the foundation for my professional success over the past thirty-some years. As a citizen of this great democracy, I am deeply concerned that our public school systems around the country—preeminent guardians of our democratic principles—are carrying out their critical educational missions in increasingly perilous times—characterized by aggressive, often-unprincipled competitors and ever-more-vociferous critics fostering distrust and skepticism. Never has the need for high-impact school board leadership and strong board-superintendent governing partnerships been greater. Yet a continuing number of school board members begin their terms ill-prepared to govern at a high level, and dedicated, bright administrators continue to assume the superintendency ill-prepared to build the close, productive, and enduring partnerships with the board that are critical to their success as district chief executives.

Meeting the challenges on the horizon will require the strong leadership of what I have described in the foregoing pages as the Strategic Governing Team: the board of education, the superintendent, and the senior administrators reporting to the superintendent. In order for the Strategic Governing Team to succeed in carrying out its leadership role, the board must be a well-developed governing body with a clearly defined role, a well-designed structure, and detailed processes for board engagement in shaping governing decisions and judgments. The team must also include a truly board-savvy superintendent who is highly knowledgeable about every aspect of the governing function, makes governing a top executive priority, and is passionately committed to strong board leadership and active collaboration with the board. And the senior administrative team must be well-prepared to support the governing function. I am confident that school board members, superintendents, and senior administrators who aspire to be superintendents can put the practical, thoroughly tested wisdom I share in this book into actual practice in building Strategic Governing Teams that are capable of meeting the challenges ahead.

I wish you well on your never-ending governing journey, and I fervently hope that you capitalize on the guidance I share in the foregoing pages to transform the challenges facing your districts into opportunities to more fully achieve your educational mission in the communities you serve.

ABOUT THE AUTHOR

President and CEO of Doug Eadie & Company, **Doug Eadie**, has—over the past thirty years—helped over five hundred public and nonprofit organizations, including many school boards and superintendents, to build their boards' capacity to do high-impact governing work and to develop rock-solid board-superintendent working relationships. Doug is the author of twenty-one books in addition to *Building a High-Impact Board-Superintendent Partnership*, including *Governing at the Top* and *Five Habits of High-Impact School Boards*, and has authored over one hundred articles on board and chief executive leadership and board–chief executive relations. He administers and writes for a popular blog for public school leaders, www.boardsavvysuperintendent.com. Before founding Doug Eadie & Company, Doug served in a number of senior executive positions in the nonprofit sector and as a Peace Corps teacher in Addis Ababa, Ethiopia, for three years. A Phi Beta Kappa graduate of the University of Illinois at Champaign-Urbana, Doug was awarded a master of science degree in management by the Weatherhead School of Case Western Reserve University.

www.ingramcontent.com/pod-product-compliance
Lightning Source LLC
Chambersburg PA
CBHW030142240426
43672CB00005B/234